KNIFER

RONNIE THOMPSON

Copyright © 2011 Ronnie Thompson

The right of Ronnie Thompson to be identified as the Author of
the Work has been asserted by him in accordance with the
Copyright, Designs and Patents Act 1988.

First published in trade paperback in 2011
by HEADLINE REVIEW
An imprint of Headline Publishing Group

First published in paperback in 2011
by HEADLINE REVIEW

1

Every effort has been made to fulfil requirements with regard to
reproducing copyright material. The author and publisher will be
glad to rectify any omissions at the earliest opportunity.

Cataloguing in Publication Data is available from the British Library

ISBN 978 0 7553 1989 3

Typeset in ZapfElliptical by Avon DataSet Ltd,
Bidford on Avon, Warwickshire

Printed in the UK by CPI Mackays, Chatham, ME5 8TD

Headline's policy is to use papers that are natural, renewable and
recyclable products and made from wood grown in sustainable
forests. The logging and manufacturing processes are expected to
conform to the environmental regulations of the country of origin.

HEADLINE PUBLISHING GROUP
An Hachette UK Company
338 Euston Road
London NW1 3BH

www.headline.co.uk
www.hachette.co.uk

CONTENTS

AUTHOR'S NOTE

Everything in this book is real. Cain Thomas is a fictional character inspired by the many teenage criminals and juvenile prisoners I have encountered in my time as a prison officer. All characters are fictitious and any similarity to real persons is entirely coincidental. But make no mistake – this is how it is. THIS IS WHAT REALLY GOES ON . . .

HOODIE

I can't say I know what it's like to be a kid. For as long as I can remember it's been a fucking war zone. My name is Cain Thomas, I'm twenty-three years old and by the age of fifteen, I was in prison for killing someone.

You see the stuff on the news about knife crime and hoodies, but that ain't the half of it. Believe. Drugs, violence, rape and murder. It's all there. Young people are guilty of those crimes.

I want to tell you about me and my life as a drug addict and criminal. You don't get to hear much about teenagers in prison – the odd thing, maybe, but not what really goes on.

I had a nightmare start to life. I don't mean to wallow

in self-pity. It's just the way it is. I'm not blaming every-thing on my upbringing. I'm accountable for my actions. But did it play a part in who I became? I'll let you make your own mind up.

I'm not going to beat around the bush when I tell you how it was. There's no point in that. I'm going to explain everything without holding back. That's the only way you'll get to step in my shoes for a short while. Some of this is difficult for me to talk about, so I've no doubt it will be difficult for you to read.

Drugs, knives, robbing, beating, abuse, prison life and practically every other vicious crime you can think of will be spoken about. All I ask is that, when you read this, try and remember that I'm talking about people under the age of eighteen. Most of you will call them kids. I can't.

I didn't live the life of a regular child. It was something different altogether.

TRIPPING

My fist was clenched hard. Fucking hard. I was ready to batter the screws.

'It's bang up, Thomas, you've had more than enough time to eat. Back to your cell.'

I ain't going nowhere. I sat in silence, so did the other seven lads I was with. One, two, then three screws slowly walked to our table. My plate of chips was stone cold. I'd not eaten a thing. Never could when I was focussing on knocking someone out.

There were forty-five cons on my Unit. They called us trainees. Political bullshit. That pissed us off. Meant they didn't take us seriously. We were serious and they were gonna find out just how serious. I was a convic'

A prisoner. And the eight of us were going to show them.

My heart pumped hard. It was ready to jump out of my chest. Serious.

'Thomas, I said . . .'

'Why you singling me out, fool? You're a fool, bruv,' I barked.

'It's you and the rest of your friends. You got to go, so let's not make this difficult.'

I jumped out of my chair and squared up to him. Even at sixteen I was over six-feet tall and big build.

'Yeah, what the fuck you gonna do?'

He didn't flinch. 'You know what I'll do, so move.'

My crew jeered at him.

'Do him, cuz. Fuck him up,' shouted Vic.

'Don't be stupid, Cain,' the screw said.

'Cain now, is it? Cain when you're shitting it; Thomas when you're bullying.'

The two other screws were getting closer to me. They were edging forward, thinking I hadn't noticed. I'd been bent up enough times to realise what they had planned. Stupid.

I stepped away from the table to give myself the room to fight. I did it slowly. They didn't notice. They figured I might put up a bit of a struggle once they'd got their hands on me. But no way were any of them cunts putting their hands on me. This was war. I was ready. I'm ready.

... are ready. This is going off.

... around; the boys were curling their lips,

4

clenching their fists. They had my back. We could take on any cunt.

He edged closer again. He moved to stand sideways. He was getting into his war stance. Ready to grab. Take me down. Never. The other two got tight in next to him. Three of them about to pounce. FUCK THAT.

BANG!

I smashed him so fucking hard in the face I swear he left his feet.

Didn't fucking expect that, did he? The cheers were instant as my boys jumped to their feet and screamed and yelled; their plates flew, the table turned. The screw I hit lay knocked out on the deck. One of the others dived for the alarm bell. Bang. The sirens were blaring. The troops were on their way.

Three boys got to work on the screw lying on the deck, stamping on him. Kids, yeah? Trainees? Fuck that. Prisoners. Convicts. They'll see.

Vic and I got on to the screw who hit the alarm bell. Coward tried to run. No chance. Vic and I smashed him to the ground. Stamped, jumped, whacked. Manning, the third screw, banged a couple of the boys down. Vic grabbed a chair and wrapped it around the back of his nut. Did nothing to him. I swear that man was the fucking terminator.

Two or three other boys fell. My man was barely conscious so I joined the take down of the terminator. Lions on a buffalo. This one didn't fall easily.

I felt a crack to the back of my head that nearly

knocked me off my feet. A handful more screws came in. With three of their comrades down, they weren't here to chat. One thing we had in common.

Before I'd even turned around, my boys had flattened him. A female screw came in too. What the fuck? No sooner had she arrived, than her nose was gushing with blood. More and more were coming, but all we did was keep stamping on the screws who were down. Let them know they were hurt. Show them what we'll do.

Their tactics changed. Rescue the damned. It wasn't a case of trying to drag us down; they just wanted to get their own back to safety. Several of them had taken a fucking shoeing. Believe. Vic was stamping down hard. Harder than I'd ever seen. He had blood in mind. He wanted to kill some cunt.

One by one, they got saved. As soon as we realised they were on the run, we knew we'd taken the place. But the one under Vic's feet was feeling no mercy. It was pointless; we had control. Vic – a mad man.

'Vic, let him go, cuz, fuck!'

The look in his eye was bad. BAD. There was one screw left, soaked in the blood from his own injuries, unable to fight back. I didn't feel sorry for him. Had too much anger. Too much fight. But it didn't feel right. Vic was going crazy. Too crazy.

I shoved him off, hard. All the others had retreated, including the rescuing screws. Partnership at its worst. They'd left him there to be killed. And that's what would have happened to him. No word of a lie. Death.

'Get out, you fucking pig!' I screamed.

He tried to get to his feet, but couldn't. Vic wanted a piece of him again.

'Fuck off, Vic,' I shoved him hard. He didn't like that. Row in the ranks. Not good.

'Get out, you fat fuck.' I kicked the screw in the arse as he tried to get to his feet. 'This Unit is mine.'

He managed to scramble away and out of the room.

'CLEAR,' shouted a screw at the gate. He locked us in. We'd won. We'd taken the sowsh and dining hall. They couldn't control us.

'BLUT, BLUT, BLUT,' we all shouted.

All the screws stood by the gate and watched us, so we gave them a show. The opposite side of the room was all bars and glass. Bang. Every fucking piece was smashed. Every fucking piece.

We busted up all the tables and chairs, and got ourselves some decent weapons at the same time.

The servery still had some cold dinner in it, so we chucked all of that through the gate at the screws. It was a scream; we were pissing ourselves. Chips, cold cod with wet breadcrumbs and beans. FUCK! The beans did the trick.

We dragged over all the tables and broken chairs, piling them up at the gates. Barricading ourselves in nice and tight.

The store cupboard was locked, so we huddled together and kept charging at it until it gave way. It was a mishmash of all-sorts because we used the dinner hall for sowsh and kit change as well as meals. It was a pretty big room for the amount of us on the Unit – eight that dinner time. The cupboard held all our games, toys and clean kit. The PlayStations and Xboxes were all taken out and smashed, and thrown next to the rest of the barricade. TVs, games, DVDs, table-tennis tables and the bats – the fucking lot came out and was destroyed. The kit came out next: tracksuits, bed stuff, pants. It all went on top of the other shit.

Once we'd cleared the cupboard we saw the vent. There was a metal cage over the top and it was just begging to be broken off. Funny thing was, we were pissing ourselves. Didn't feel fuck all about what we were doing. Just humour. Our time of importance.

Vic was becoming the dictator, which was getting on my tits. I wanted to bang the fool but I was biting my tongue. He was shoving Apples around for no fucking reason. Apples was a good boy. One of your own. Fucking geezer. A comic. Always up for the crack. Would be by your side when you needed him. And Vic was starting to take liberties, talking to him like a cunt.

'Apples, come over here, you nigger.' Trash talking.

'The fuck you talking to like that?' I said to him. Vic and I are white. Fucking idiot needs to learn some respect.

'What? Talk to me like that again, blood, you'll fucking get it.' He stepped up.

Nose to nose, I was ready to smash him.

'You two, leave it!' Apples said, grinning from ear to ear, trying to make light of it.

Vic and I eyeballed each other for a few seconds before we touched fists.

'Safe,' we said reluctantly to each other.

We got to work ripping the vent open. We took it in turns whacking it with our table-leg weapons. It didn't take long to move.

'Thomas? Cain? CAIN?' I heard someone shouting. One of the screws. I walked out to see what he wanted. All my boys followed. I got pretty close to the gate, staring at the screw the whole time. He was sweating. Looking agitated. Nervous. I fucking wasn't. He just stood there.

'What you calling me for, cunt?' I spat.

'Cain . . .'

'Don't call me that, you pig. I'm a fucking convict called Thomas, so don't start getting all gay on me now, just cos I bashed you fucking batty boys and now you're wanting to be nice, no, be gay.'

'It's not like that . . .'

'Yeah, fucking gay cunt. That's what you are. A fucking cock-taking batty boy. Bet you only work here so you can touch young men, you fucking ANIMAL,' I screamed at him. The boys laughed.

'Thing is, we don't know what it is you want. Why are you doing this?'

Too much bang up, because you lazy cunts are always going sick.

'Respect, you piece of shit. Fucking respect.'

He took a deep breath. Seemed to calm himself. 'Thing is, Cain . . .'

'Thomas, CUNT.'

'Sorry, Thomas. There's things we can do, honestly there is. But there's rules . . .'

'Fuck your rules. Suck ya mum.' I stormed off. Didn't want to listen to his petty bullshit.

We all went back into the cupboard and took a look at the vent. It was going to be a tight fit, but we realised we could climb up it. Didn't have a fucking clue where it led to. Vic jumped in first, with me close behind.

It was pitch black and fucking small. I had to practically dislocate my shoulders to squeeze my thick frame into the space. Once I'd forced myself in, lying horizontally – I could see that it went upwards. Vic was already out of sight.

I wiggled my hips from side to side and pushed with my toes. I moved forward. Slowly. I curled myself around the sharp bend. I was soaked with sweat. Totally saturated. Finally, it was a relief to be on my feet.

'Hurry up, Fatty!' Apples was behind me.

'Think I need a piss. In fact I might just take one now . . .'

'NO! NO!'

We both laughed.

I managed to put my knees and feet on opposite sides of the ducting. I started my ascent. I couldn't even see Vic. Rat. Drainpipe. Vermin.

It was a long way up. Never fucking ending. There were several twists, turns and climbs. But it was going up, which was great. There was only one place it could lead. The roof.

I saw some light ahead. Not light exactly, but evening dusk. I edged closer, inch by inch. As I poked my head out, I saw Vic shouting and waving his weapon around. My hand was aching like fuck from carrying my table leg all the way up there.

'Took ya time, blood.'

I didn't bother answering him. The roof was flat, so we could run around and do what the fuck we wanted up there. We were two storeys up – felt like the king of the jailhouse castle.

There was a group of screws gathered below. They were running around, talking on their radios, pointing, planning. Fuck knows what they were up to. Vic was shouting down some raw abuse. Dirty.

Apples was trying to get out, but had lost his energy. 'I beg you, big man, help me out!'

I went over and pulled him out of the shaft and on to the roof. The other lads followed, one at a time. And there we were. Roof-top protesters.

It was getting cold. We'd been up there for fucking ages and we hadn't really said anything to each other for the last hour. I looked around at the other lads.

I was losing the fight inside. I'd been losing my edge for a while. I was playing at being bad. Truth is, I wasn't finding that shit at all natural or enjoyable any more. I'd gone against the system for so long. I'd been in prison

11

over a year and hadn't had a single day where I'd not argued with someone or something. I sat there, not really knowing why I was up there or what I was arguing about. It was a funny place to have them thoughts and feelings.

I looked around and most of the other lads were huddled together, looking tired, hungry and cold. Vic didn't – he wanted to go on and on.

'I'm fucking freezing, I'm getting down.' Apples had had enough.

'You're going nowhere, blood,' Vic ordered.

'Fuck that, man, this is bollocks. I wanna go, innit.' He got up and walked to the edge.

'Sit the fuck back down,' shouted Vic.

Apples gave him a dirty look and ignored him. I stood up. I could see Vic wasn't going to leave it. I had no choice. No choice. Fuck. We were right in the middle of the roof.

Apples walked to the edge. 'Come get me, I wanna come down, Boss,' he shouted to the screws below.

Vic tightened his grip around his weapon and started running for him. I ran after him.

'Apples, LOOK OUT,' I yelled.

BANG! Vic cracked him around the back of the head. He stumbled forward, screaming in pain, he was inches from the edge. Inches. I was on Vic but he spun around and smashed me in the guts, taking me off my feet. I curled up in pain. The other boys watched. Fucking watched. Cowards. Or was I the coward?

'You wanna go, nigger, then go.' He kicked Apples in the back as hard as he could.

Apples flew off the edge.

'NO!' I screamed.

Vic turned to me with a dirty, evil grin spreading across his face. 'Time for me to take back what's mine, you fucking pussy-hole. You've had your chance at playing the big man. You're fuck all, and now I'm gonna smash you up, fool.'

My stomach was charging its way up my throat. I tried to stand, but failed. I was in too much pain. Vic edged towards me with his weapon raised. He was ready to batter me. Take me down. Fuck me up. I was in agony. Physically I couldn't stand.

Apples. Fuck.

I looked over at the other boys. None of them looked like they were going to stop him. Looked more like they wanted to fucking run.

I breathed deep and fast, trying to get myself ready to fight. Once again I failed to get to my feet. Vic looked down on me, weapon raised. I stared at him straight in the eyes. It was out of my hands. I was on that roof, sixteen years old and my short, hedonistic life was about to come to a violent end. Everything flashed before me. EVERYTHING. How the hell had my life got to this?

STAINED

Everywhere I went, I kept my lock-knife on me. It had a bronze-gold handle and a four-inch blade. It folded in half nicely and I carried it in my sock. Eight years old and I was carrying a knife.

I needed it for my protection.

It would rub like a bastard. The skin on my ankle was full of pus and infection. As I always carried it, the skin never had a chance to scab up and heal. Plus, I wasn't the cleanest of boys. Never washed unless I was forced to.

My foster mother was a cunt. I thought it then and still do now. Cunt. She was an image-conscious, middle-class fool who knew the square root of fuck all. All she was bothered about was what the neighbours thought.

She didn't need to foster but she thought it looked good to help the needy. But she never had the time of day for anyone except her sad, useless self. I was the trophy 'damaged child' that she told everyone she'd saved. What a load of bollocks. She was probably my tenth or eleventh placement in eight years. I had so many, I can't remember them all. But I fucking remember that one. Evil.

I'd been in care my whole life. I was taken from my mother at birth. I was one of eight kids that she had taken away. She was a junkie. A junkie that liked to fuck without protection. Even though she knew she'd have her kid taken away at the delivery suite, she still did it. I wasn't the last one either. Number five, I think. Not that I think too much about it. It would drive me mental. Insane.

I never knew what it was like to be in a family. I wasn't adopted. Don't know why. You have a window of opportunity and then, once you get past a certain age, you've had it. A life of homes and second-rate families who do it for money. Sure, there're some beautiful people out there who do it for love. So I'm told. I never seen it. On the news, yeah. In real life. Never.

But then, I wasn't a nice kid. Not one bit. I was angry. Think I was born that way. Angry at the fucking world. It was a preservation thing. I knew the shit I was headed for, so I thought I'd be as fucking nasty as I could along the way. That way, no one would fuck with me. All I achieved, though, was getting moved from one house to the next. No one could handle me.

And then I found myself at eight years old living with the Sick family. That's how I remember all of them: SICK.

It was dark, about seven o'clock. I was only supposed to hang out in the street – the cul-de-sac where I lived. Fuck that. I went everywhere on that push bike. Robbing sweets, nicking toys. I should have been home hours earlier. I didn't give a shit.

I rode around the back of the house and threw my bike on the floor.

'Cain, at last! Where the hell have you been?' Mrs Sick asked.

I didn't even bother to answer. I didn't actually talk back that much. I just looked at her standing there with stupid curlers in her thick, wiry hair and laughed in her face.

'Don't you laugh at me, you little shit. Put your bike away.'

I walked past her, saying fuck all. Her husband sat at the table, pretending to read the paper. He said nothing. Think he hated her as much as I did, but was too scared to say anything.

'You going to let him talk to me like that?' she said to him.

'I've not said anything.' Which I hadn't. Stupid cow.

He buried his head deeper into his paper. Weak individual. Bastard.

'There's some quiche and bread in the fridge,' she said, with a smile on her face. I fucking detested eggs. Quiche made me vomit. But that's what she gave me all the fucking time. I opened the fridge and saw there were only a couple of broken pieces left and some dry bread. I was hungry. Very hungry.

'There anything else?'

'No, there isn't. You get what you're given. Now eat it.' Fucking witch did scare me at times.

I was a horrible little bugger but I was still only eight years old. She sat there and made me eat it. There was cold rice-pudding for afters. The skin made me feel sick. I ate a bowl of cold skin, I kid you not. I think that was her way of serving me a little retribution for my insolence. I gagged with every mouthful. Felt sick to my stomach. But she sat right next to me, and made me finish every single mouthful. Disgusting. So was the food.

'I'm going to run you a bath. You stink like a polecat, you filthy little animal.' Lovely lady.

'Don't want one.' I didn't for good reason. Hated being seen naked and she always made the water fucking boiling hot.

'That wasn't a question.'

I ran up to my room and slammed the door shut. I heard the tapping of the pipes and the dull vibrating sound of the bath beginning to fill. I pulled out my drawing pad that I kept under my bed.

I loved drawing. Cartoon characters mainly. I used to copy stuff when I'd first started, but now I was making up my own stories. I had a terrific imagination and was a decent little artist. Think it was the only thing I was good at. It was definitely the only thing I enjoyed. I used to lose myself in my drawings for hours.

I could create whole other worlds. Craft this parallel universe, where I was in control. There would be occasional characters of love and kindness but most of them were extreme punishers. It was a place where I could play out my fantasies of hurting people who had hurt me. I had some awful crazy thoughts.

'CAIN, GET DOWN HERE, YOUR BATH'S READY.' Battleaxe bitch.

I tried to ignore her, hoping she'd go away.

'DON'T MAKE ME COME UP THERE.' But she never did.

I closed my pad and carefully placed it under my bed and I went downstairs. Silly old hag still had her ridiculous curlers in. I walked into the bathroom and she just stood there, staring. I waited for her to go. I didn't want her seeing me naked. Didn't want anyone seeing me naked. I looked at her right in the eye, hoping she'd get the message. She just grinned at me.

'Right, get in.'

I just stared. FUCK OFF. Still she stood there.

'I said get your clothes off and get in . . .' Don't fucking touch me.

I kicked her hard in the shin.

'OUCH! Why you . . . Andrew? ANDREW, this little sod just kicked me!' she bellowed to her pussy-hole husband.

I didn't smile but on the inside I was pissing myself.

Tired, out of breath and agitated by the confrontation, Daddy Sick came to the bathroom.

'Cain, look, don't hit your mother.'

'She's not my mother,' I said.

'All that I provide for you, you little shit. You'd be in the gutter without me. No one wanted you, so show some respect.'

I just stared. I hated her. Looking back, I've no clue how she was even allowed to foster. Actually, that's a lie. She had an air-freshened semi, a boring Hyundai on the drive and a moustache-wearing ponce for a husband. And a biological son. Animal. FUCKING ANIMAL is what he is.

On paper, she looked perfect. On paper.

'Just get in the bath, Cain. Then there's no arguments.'

He was a pacifier, I'll give him that. But for the wrong reasons. A fucking coward.

'I just want to get in on my own.'

He looked at Sick Witch, 'Come on, love, let's leave him.'

She gave me dagger stares and left.

I shut the door, but didn't lock it. I pulled off my T-shirt. I remember looking down at my body, thinking I had a torso full of muscles. When the truth is, I was a skinny runt who barely ate. My body was full of bruises and scratches and looked tanned with dirt. I hated washing. Hated being naked. Hated being looked at.

I took off my jogging bottoms and it was then that I realised I'd forgotten to leave my knife in my bedroom.

That fat cow would go through my clothes. I put the knife inside one of the socks and then put that inside the T-shirt, which I then put inside the jogging bottoms. All in a heap, so you couldn't see it. I pulled my pants off and the door burst open. Fuck. I covered myself up.

'I've come to get your dirty clothes,' she said.

'Err, no, I, err, want them for tomorrow,' I was panicking.

'OK, I will wash them, then. You bloody stink, boy.'

She bent down to pick up my clothes.

'LEAVE THEM ALONE, YOU CUNT,' I screamed.

A lovely mouth. I screamed and screamed and screamed. I was foaming at the mouth. I was shocked by the level of noise that came out of my scrawny body. It was the only way I could stop her, get her to listen.

She wasn't taking away my knife. It was my protection. My fucking saviour. Bitch.

Andrew came running in. Probably the first time he'd run in years.

'What the hell is going on?' he asked.

I caught my breath and opened my eyes to look at her. She was shocked, almost scared, by my outrage. By my violent shouting. I caught my breath and started to calm a little.

'I just came to get his dirty clothes,' she whispered. 'He's crazy. Mad.'

'I want them; I don't want her taking them,' I said, quietly.

Explosion, then mouse-like.

'Just leave it, love; it'll keep until tomorrow,' he said.

The mood changed – slightly. She regained her composure and started to walk out. But she couldn't leave it.

'Get in and wash, you dirty little rat, you stink.' She pushed me fucking hard so I fell into the water.

'ARRGGHH,' I screamed. Kettle hot. Cunt.

Sadistic bitch laughed. She'd regained her control. Well done, you fucking bully.

I don't know what time it was exactly but it was fucking late. Midnight, one, something like that. Them two were snoring like pigs. I wasn't sleeping that well. Always suffered bad with insomnia.

I was sat up in bed, working on Shark-Boy, one of my characters – a boy who turned into a half shark, half boy creature once he was fully submerged in water. He lived in a seaside town and would hit the waves and take on all the pirates in the sea. A superhero. My superhero. I was Shark-Boy. Think I got that from her fucking baths. I wanted to fucking eat her.

I'd been working on a few sketches all evening. I was almost happy; submersed in my drawings. I had found a bit of comfort and bliss. No noise. No fights. Just me, my drawings and my imagination. Amazing.

I didn't hear the door open, but I heard it close. It was done quietly but the sound was enough to make me turn around. Fuck. Her son, Sicko, was standing inside my room. He had an evil smile. A nasty fucking smile.

He was nineteen years old. A fat bastard covered in

zits. He was tall and big, but still had a babyish look about him. He had a bum-fluff chin, unkempt hair and a repulsive body. I never really saw him with friends. He was at college doing computers or something – can't remember, just know he was a fucking geek.

He walked slowly over to my bed and sat down. He didn't say anything, just smiled. I curled up tight at the end of the bed. I wanted to create as much distance between him and me as I could. He stared at me for a while, breathing heavily.

'What you been doing, Cain? You should be asleep at this time.' He was slurring his words. Pissed up.

'Nothing.'

Fuck off.

'What's that?' He noticed my pad.

'It's nothing.' I grabbed it and pulled it towards me.

'Let me see?' he said, smiling.

'No, leave me alone.'

His smile dropped. He instantly looked more serious.

'When I ask, you fucking give. Let me see it.'

I ignored him and pulled it tighter towards me. It was the one and only thing that was unequivocally mine. And that cunt wasn't going to get his fat, greasy paws on it.

He moved in quickly, trying to snatch it out of my hand. I dodged him.

'Give it to me, you little shit.'

I didn't.

He bundled on top of me. I still wouldn't give it to him, so he smacked me in the face.

'ARGH,' I screamed.

'Shut your fucking mouth, you'll wake Mum and Dad.'

He managed to get the pad in his grasp. He didn't get his fat, repulsive self off me, though. I was crumpled underneath him as he looked at my drawings.

'Shark-Boy!? Who the fuck is Shark-Boy?'

'Give it back.'

'You stupid little twat, these are shit.'

I hated him. I wanted to kill him. He threw my pad over his shoulder, so it fell on the floor. He put his hand on my leg. The inside of it, near my groin.

'You've not really been drawing them. No, I know what you've been doing. Waiting up for me – that's it, isn't it?'

He moved in closer, his breath fucking stank. Stank of booze. Dirty, fat pig.

'No, get off me. Get off me!' I said a little louder.

He dug me in the ribs.

'Keep your fucking mouth quiet!'

I shat myself. He scared me. Fucking scared me. He put his hands inside my pyjamas. I froze for a second. No way was that happening again. I'd got that knife for a reason. It was just in case that dirty, kid-raping cunt came at me again.

I slipped my hand under my pillow so quick he didn't notice. He was too busy salivating, the scum. SCUM. I flicked out the blade and thrust it deep into the side of his gut. BANG. Have that!

I froze for a second. He heard the stab. Don't think he

was sure he felt it. He looked at me in the eyes. I didn't look away once.

He looked down at his gut and saw his blood seeping out.

'What have you done?' Fat cunt took his hands back to himself.

Bang. BANG! Twice more I stabbed him. He fell off my bed and began to scream. I dived on him and managed to get the blade in him once more. He got hold of me, trying to stop me from stabbing him again. We were both soaked in his blood. There was so much blood. I wanted to kill him. I wanted him dead. DEAD.

I didn't hear the door open. I didn't even feel anything. It was as if I was flying. I was hovering over the disgusting, raping cunt. Looking down on him squirming in his own blood. Fearing for his life. Dying in front of me. Scared. Vulnerable. How do you think I felt when you raped me all those times? Yeah, RAPED ME.

That image of him was better than any drawing I could produce.

I got that knife. I couldn't take another night-time visit. I wouldn't take it. I kept it on me the whole time. Near me. Just in case it happened again.

His fat body was his protection. Flubber wounds, that's all. Bled like a bitch.

Andrew was holding me off his paedophile son. His mum dived down to comfort him. Baby nonce, my poor baby nonce.

* * *

There were no police called. Nothing. They didn't want anyone to find out about it. Did they know what was going on? Doubt it. But they did after that. The fear that I might taint their reputation was too much to bear. The thought of Sicko going to prison was too much for them. Social services were called and I was taken away. I was a nasty kid. I told you that. Did they believe me? No chance.

Mrs Sick gave it the, 'We don't want to take this further, we are kind people. But we can no longer have that boy in our house.' With her upstanding appearance and demeanour, she had them eating out of her palms. I was the nasty, vicious, stabbing child. The eight-year-old animal.

That was the last family I lived with. From then on it was homes and units full of kids just like me. Beyond foster care.

Stabbing that fool empowered me. I felt good. Tough. Like I could kill someone. I decided then, no one would ever fuck with me again.

ADRIAN MOLE (ON SKUNK
AND WITH A BLADE)

I liked being by the sea, that's for sure. It was the only
good thing about the place. It wasn't some million-
aire's paradise town, though. No way. Rat-infested
kebab shops, shitty, old arcade games and the pissed-up
unemployed loitering everywhere. It was a recipe for
violence. Still, the tourists flocked there as soon as there
was a bit of sun. Funny thing was, the place may have
been a shithole but the beach was class. Huge and pure
sand. Shame that prettiness couldn't have rubbed off on
the rest of the town.

It was fucking boiling hot for June. The sun came early.
TJ, Radman and I were riding around town in baggy jeans
and hooded jumpers. Hoods up. I was sweating my

bollocks off, but didn't care. How I looked and carried myself was all that mattered. TJ and Radman were both fifteen. I was going to turn fourteen soon.

I had met Radman at Clear-View House. That was where I was living. Me and about ten other kids. Boys and girls. Loved that. Radman was also a resident. I'd been there six, nearly seven months. It was all right. It was a place for kids who had nowhere else to go. We had teachers there, too. Eat, sleep and school there. Well, supposedly school.

Radman didn't give a fuck. All he was interested in was riding his BMX. Shit hot on it, hence his nickname. He was pretty quiet but fucking hard as nails. I'd seen him knock out teachers, one after the other. Bam. Fuck knows why they worked there. Fighting with us was standard practice. Still, they turned up. Most of them.

TJ went to the local comprehensive. He hardly ever showed up. When he did, he was excluded more often than not. Never on a permanent basis. Geezer was in year eleven, so it was pointless. They knew they'd see the back of him soon, so they didn't give a fuck.

We were riding through town going to get a Maccy-D's. We'd got hold of some mega strong skunk. Blew your fucking head off. Made me hallucinate and all sorts. Once that passed, we got the mega munchies.

The pavement was pretty full, even though it was a Wednesday. All of us should have been in class. Fuck that. It was busy because the sun was out. Soon as that happened, people came running.

We were knocking folk out of the way as we went. Whines and screams, but we just carried on forward. Some woman got right in front of me – wallop, over she went. I nearly fell off my bike.

'Watch where you're going, you stupid little twat,' her man, about forty, shouted.

I jumped off my bike and ran right up to him. Radman and TJ behind me.

'Fuck did you say, bruv? Huh?' Nose to nose.

Not even fourteen and I was already five nine or ten. Big boy. Looked older than my years. He stepped back, worried. All the bystanders just watched.

'I don't want no trouble, lads, just my missus is pregnant, you know?'

'Bet it's not yours, you cunt,' TJ piped up.

'You said shit to the wrong person,' I said.

Radman got his mobile phone out and hit record.

'Come on, lads, there's no need for this.'

TJ and I got closer to him. His woman got to her feet.

'Fuck off, you horrible bastards, leave us alone!'

'Shut ya mouth, you sket,' TJ said.

'Come on, say something now, you fat cunt, instead of hiding behind big guts here.'

'Boys, please . . .'

TJ and I were on him. We cracked him to the ground and stamped down hard.

'ARRGGHH, STOP, YOU FUCKING ANIMALS,' screamed the woman.

Radman filmed it all. Not one person stopped to help.

People stared. Some disgusted. But a random beating wasn't an unusual event. OK, that was particularly nasty. But it was a terrible place, you get me?

We left the man crying. We ran to our BMXs, laughing all the way. We biked off as fast as we could.

'Excuse me, lads, no bikes in here.' We never left our bikes outside Maccy-D's. Fucking things would have been nicked in a shot, no question. Every time we went some joker in a uniform would challenge us.

We gave him death stares, then turned away from him and carried on chatting, queuing for food. Shit, I was hungry. I was mashed. And fighting that fool had made me hungrier.

'Lads, you're going to have to take them outside.'

'Carry on about your fucking business, you joker,' TJ shouted.

'Look, the manager has told me . . .'

'Grow some balls, bruv, and tell him to fuck off.'

The guy stood there sweating it. He didn't know what to do. He looked over at his manager behind the counter. We all watched his reaction. Fuck. Another fight was brewing and all I wanted was some food. Some fucking food. Hunger was a problem my whole life. Seemed to spend every waking hour yearning for food, I swear.

The manager held up his hands in a defeated gesture. He'd seen the look on our faces. He knew we'd have smashed his shop to pieces. He knew to leave us the fuck alone. Good.

Finally we got to the counter. 'Quarter Pounder with cheese meal, large, with a Coke; a Big Mac, six chicken nuggets and a chocolate doughnut. And barbecue sauce. Give me bear amounts, I beg you.' The boys laughed at the amount I ordered.

We got our food and went to find a table. Place was pretty full. There was a table to one side with a couple of Star Wars geeks. Looked like computer nerds. Fucking hated computer nerds. Sick.

We rolled over to them. They looked up, saying nothing, and moved away. Fast. We sat down and got stuck into the grub. It tasted divine. The munchy pangs were banging. True.

Radman got his phone out and played back the fight. The volume was loud, too. A few people looked around at us. We all pissed ourselves as we watched our handiwork. Maniacs. Careless. Cruel. It was quarter past twelve. We needed to get to TJ's school before the end of lunch break.

There were a few kids out the front smoking fags when we got there.

'You lot want any skunk?' TJ asked.

'Better than the last shit?' asked one of the boys.

'Yeah, big time. Cain, get it out.'

I pulled out a huge bag and passed it over. He looked and smelt it.

'That's a bear bag, man! Shit, I'll have a quarter.'

'Money now, no ticking. Boys are taking the piss.' Radman was sick of little bastards not paying.

'Sweet, big man.' He pulled out a wad of cash. He was fourteen. Loads of money. Everyone was on the rob. This fool used to buy it off us and then take a load, and shift the rest on to younger kids for more dough. He handed over the money to Radman and the rest of the gear back to me.

'Bless,' Radman said, as he was passed the cash.

We rode through the front gates of the school and there were a few boys and short-skirt skets milling about. The midday assistants and teachers we could see said fuck all to us. Too scared. There we were, riding through school on our BMXs – hoods up, stoned and carrying gear.

We got near the playground and saw some kid walking on his own.

'You. Come here,' TJ said to him.

The boy came over, shitting himself.

'You seen Ox?'

'Erm . . .'

'Come on, you little cunt, you seen him?'

'Yeah, he's behind the trees at the back of the tennis courts. He's with . . .'

We didn't wait to hear what he had to say.

'Cunt better have our money.' Radman was interested in our profit.

We did a lot of drug dealing. And we had a load of cash all the time. Radman was the businessman, TJ the nutty boy and me the crazy apprentice.

Ox was a big sixth former. Played second row for the county's rugby team. Looked like he was going to go pro.

I guess you can work out why he was called what he was called. Believe. The geezer was fucking huge. HUGE.

Big or not, the cunt owed us money.

We cycled around the back of the building until we came to the playground and tennis courts. All the kids looked at us with fearful eyes and got out of our way as we cycled through.

The tennis courts were concrete and had netball lines marked out as well, and five-a-side football nets were set up. A load of boys were playing. The sides and back of the courts were surrounded by fifteen-foot conifer trees, so dense you couldn't see through them.

We got to the side of the court and put our bikes down.

'You. Oi, KID. Come here,' I shouted. Called him kid but the boy was older than me.

'Watch these bikes. Anything happens to them, I'll mash you up.'

He nodded in fear.

We crept up the side, trying to be as quiet as we could. Ox was probably around there getting high. That's the only reason to go there. That or make out with some sket.

'I'm gonna fuck him up.' TJ was mad. Furious.

We got to the back of the court and the three of us peeked around the corner. There he was, the big ugly bastard. He was making out with some girl. Heavy breathing like a hairy ape. Couldn't see her properly. Just hands, half a titty and a skirt that was pulled up over her hips. Her head was pushed back deep in the foliage so we couldn't see her face.

We all sniggered and looked on enjoying the show. Funny as fuck. Thought we'd take it in before collecting our debt. The girl was moaning like a porn star. True. Jenna Jameson, eat your heart out. He was grunting and slobbering like a dirty caveman. I was giggling like a girl. I was still a virgin. Had a fumble but not much else. Found it easier to insult a girl than flirt with her.

Then her face popped into view. TJ stopped laughing. Radman quietened down. I didn't. I was still pointing, finding the whole thing hilarious. I hadn't noticed their silence, not until Radman punched me in the guts.

'Shut up, man, that's TJ's fucking girl.' Ouch. Fucking ouch.

TJ was still staring. Frowning. Looking evil as they come. Shit.

'Leave it, man; we'll get that fool and his money later.' Radman tried to pull TJ away.

'Fool pays now.'

'Leave it.'

'Get the fuck off me.'

He stormed towards them; Radman and me in tow. Ox heard us coming and quickly tried to do his trousers up.

'Fuck!' he shouted as he fumbled.

Ox was too fast. Big but fast. He decked TJ with one big punch. Radman jumped in, and so did I. It was like trying to cut an oak tree with a blunt axe. TJ got to his feet and joined in. An eye gouge and some stamps to the bollocks was enough to get him to his knees. Then we smashed him in the face until he was pretty much on his back. His face was beginning to swell like the elephant man. A bit of blood, but not much. It was like his body was made out of rubber. He absorbed all the blows. But he did swell. Fuck, he was ugly. TJ jumped on top of him.

'Where's my fucking money?'

'Err, I can get it . . .' He was struggling to speak and was dribbling blood.

'You don't pay me and then you fuck my bird?'

'TJ, leave him.'

'Shut up, you fucking sket.'

I looked around at her fixing her blouse and straightening her skirt. She had bottle blonde hair, lots of make-up and a stern look. Her school uniform was turned into a hybrid of slut wear. Bitch. It was the first time I had ever seen Lily and I fancied the fuck out of her. My jaw nearly hit the ground.

TJ pulled out a knife and put it to Ox's face.

'My money, where's my fucking money?'

'Easy, put it away.' Radman stepped in.

'Get back, Radman, I swear.' TJ turned the knife on him for a second. Madman. Believe.

Radman backed off.

Ox was fumbling around with his pockets and pulled out a wad of cash.

'Take this,' Ox said.

It was more than he owed. I went over and snatched it out of his hand. TJ appeared to calm a little. Ox looked relieved. The tension was fading then – BAM! TJ stabbed the boy right in the stomach.

'ARRGGHH,' he yelled. Fucking blood everywhere. He was screaming like a pig in a slaughterhouse. Radman and I pulled TJ off him. Madman wanted to go back and stab him again. Lily screamed.

'Let's fucking go!' shouted Radman.

We all ran off except Lily. She got on her knees and stayed with Ox. We sprinted like mad. TJ was laughing – pleased with the wad of cash he had in his hand.

I stopped and looked back. Ox was moaning and holding his belly. Lily was trying her best to tend to him. She looked up and stared at me right in the eyes. I felt myself being drawn back to her. She didn't look away, not once.

'What you doing, bruv? Fuck, let's go!' Radman came back and dragged me away. All the time I couldn't stop looking at her. Trouble with a capital T was spelt out in front of me. Fact.

SO YOU WANNA BE
A GANGSTA

It was the colours that made it amazing. There were so many. That was one good thing about Clear-View, they had quality equipment. State of the art stuff. But all I was interested in was the paints, pencils and charcoals. And there were shit loads. My artwork was the only thing I cared about. The only lesson I ever attended. I still found solace in my pictures. I was nearly fifteen and Shark-Boy was still my obsession.

The piece I was working on was elaborate. It was Shark-Boy jumping out of the sea fighting with an amphibious pirate who lived under the sea. The story had evolved. The pirates were half man, half squid and were plotting to take over the world.

Not that I'd written any dialogue. I just drew and painted exotic pictures. Pens and brush, ink and charcoal – I used them all. It was comic art, like the stuff you see on *Heroes*. Loved it. It was my escapism. It took me away from my regular habits for a short while.

'Cain, that is absolutely fantastic.' Mr Pritchard was an old eccentric with a grey beard and worn-out clothes. Shit, the man took some abuse. Spat at, punched, kicked, threatened. But he never lost his temper, always stayed calm. And always fucking turned up! He was all right.

'Cheers, Boss. Been working on him for some time now.'

'You should try and develop a story or something . . .'

Radman came over and interrupted, 'Shit, Cain, that's the bollocks, mate.'

I wasn't sure if he was taking the piss. I hoped not. I would have smashed anyone for doing that. Including him.

'Yeah, cheers,' I said, sternly.

'Right, let's go, man. Got shit to do.' He changed the subject.

'Can you put this away for me, Boss?'

'Lesson isn't finished yet, Cain.'

'Is for me.'

'Cain, rules are rules.'

'I agree, but they're there to be broken.'

We walked out.

'You heard about your bedsit yet?' I asked Radman.

'Nah, fuck all. Ain't bothered, innit. I'm still here. Roof and food. BLUT, BLUT.'

Radman was nearly seventeen. Clear-View only went up to sixteen year olds. But spaces in bedsits were few and far between, so there were a few loiterers. Radman being one of them.

We got on our BMXs and road out of the gates. No one said anything. Place did have rules, but hardly anyone enforced them. They were just pleased when no one kicked off. I was in a good mood. Burying myself in Shark-Boy made me feel that way.

As we rode, I pulled out two cans of Special Brew. Big piss. Knocks your fucking head off. I passed one to Radman.

'You're fucking crazy, man. Why do you drink that shit?'

'Starts the party, bruv, starts the party!'

He took the can and we drank.

The flat was on the eleventh floor. Lifts were fucking broke, as usual, so the stairs it was. By the time I got up there, I was hanging out of my arse.

'Why couldn't that lazy cunt bring down?' I asked.

'We're lucky he's ticking it, bruv.'

We knocked on the door and some nasty-looking cunt answered, wrecked out of his nut.

'TJ in?'

The door opened further and we walked in. There was drum and bass blasting out the stereo and the place stank of piss, smoke and dirty carpets. Rough. There was about four or five people in the lounge as we entered.

There was Charlie racked up on the coffee table and bags of pills. TJ barely noticed us walk in. Lily was sitting on the sofa looking fucked out of her tiny mind.

'All right, boys. Sit.' TJ was barely able to speak.

I sat on the sofa next to Lily. She put her hand on my leg.

'Hi, sexy, it's been a while,' she whispered.

I looked up to see if TJ had noticed. He hadn't. He was too busy loading up a pipe full of crack and smoking it. He'd moved up a gear.

I didn't know whose flat it was exactly, but TJ ran his dealing from there for a 'relative'. That's all he ever told me. I never saw that relative. But I guess he or she must have existed because TJ was seventeen, and I'd seen him bully and bitchslap nutters who were twice his age. They wouldn't have taken it unless TJ had some clout. The boy was fucking hard, I ain't taking that away. Believe. He was nuts. But some of the liberties he took were over and above his level of fight.

Radman helped himself to a line of Charlie.

'When you taking me out?' Lily asked me. She was wrecked. Stoned, pissed – the fucking lot by the look of it.

'Shut up, you messer, you're with TJ. Keep your fucking noise down, he's only over there.'

But I fancied her. Yeah. Big time. More than that; she never left me alone. Once or twice I'd had a snog with her. But I didn't want to take it any further. Too scared, if I'm honest. TJ was mad and I'd seen what he could do. Fuck, he ended Ox's rugby career. Didn't kill him, but severed his abdominal muscles so badly, the geezer struggled to get out of bed, let alone run around a rugby pitch. But sometimes I couldn't resist her. I didn't have the bottle to go all the way.

I'd been having sex and didn't my dick know about it. I'd already had chlamydia and some nasty little cauliflower warts sprouting all over my helmet. Condoms weren't on my agenda. I thought they made it feel shit. I wanted pussy and didn't give a fuck about anything else. I wanted to look big. Be the man who fucked women. Big man. Cock.

Lily had something, though. Sure, she fucked around and was a right sket, but she did something to me. Why her? Fuck.

'If you don't want me, then fine. I thought you were different.'

'While you're with him, stay away.'

I didn't like TJ. I used to look up to him. But I'd grown physically and mentally and I thought he was a cunt who hid behind his contacts. We all do that to a degree. Believe. But with him it was just one step too far. And, for that, I was scared of him. Even though Radman and I were supposed to be his mates, TJ still let us know that he would do us if necessary. A power freak.

I got up and snorted a line of coke.

'Got any pills, TJ?' I asked him.

'Yeah, what you gonna do for it, big man?'

'Pay you later, innit.' God, I fucking hated him.

'Nah, boy, you gotta do more than that.'

'Who the fuck you calling boy, bruv? You're only a year older than me.'

'Nearly two,' he snapped back.

Radman jumped in, 'Can you two hear yourself?!'

TJ laughed. I didn't.

'You got any booze?' I asked.

'Lily, go get Cain some vodka.'

'He can get it himself, he knows where it is.'

He grabbed a CD case which was the first thing he could get his hands on and threw it at her. 'Don't mouth at me, you FUCKING SKET! Get him a fucking drink now, you cunt.'

I bit my lip. I wanted to smash him hard. The CD missed her face by an inch. She went out of the room.

'There.' He tossed me two pills.

Lily came back with a small bottle of cheap vodka. I washed down the two pills with it. It tasted rank and I was practically sick in my mouth. But I didn't show it. Big man. I swallowed some more.

'Ride Crew are taking the fucking piss. Mozza has been bad mouthing me. I want you and Rad to go and serve them up. Proper.'

'It's done, bruv,' I said.

I was up for a fight. The rumble was my pleasure. I felt half pissed and a little wired. I knew he wanted blood, so I was going to give it to him.

TJ loaded the pipe again, 'Give you an edge, bruv.'

He passed me the pipe and I smoked it. My first time doing crack. Not even fifteen and I was pissed, on Es, coke and crack. With a knife in my pocket and instructions to use it.

We were in the arcades playing some shit game – think it was Teenage Turtles. A fucking version of the game that was older than I was. But that was what the arcades were like in that rough, old town. Shit.

The arcades were just across the road from a kebab shop and Maccy-D's. We knew Mozza and all his fools would be around there. We went to have a game while we waited.

We'd been there fucking ages – it was about our tenth go and we couldn't get past a certain level. Money we'd pumped in there . . . Shit – lost again.

'Fucking shit game,' I shouted and started kicking it.

The steward, or whatever the geezer is called who runs the arcade, came over.

'The hell do you think you're doing? Stop that or I'll ring the police.'

We walked off. 'Suck ya mum, ya fat prick,' I shouted.

Radman wet himself. We went outside. There was a pub just to the left of the arcade. We went around the side where it was quiet so we could have a smoke but still watch the kebab shop.

I was out of my nut. Rushing like a bitch, feeling tough, then soft. Fucked. I rolled up a big, fat, skunk spliff. We smoked it quickly and I rolled another one.

'You got any rock?' I asked.

'Man, don't be a crack head. Just humour TJ. Don't go down that road, bruv. He's a fucking menace.'

But I did want to go down that road. I wanted to be the big man. I wanted to be the badass. The drugs were about looking the part. Sure. But I liked them. I can't lie. I loved being so fucked I felt nothing but euphoria. It gave me pleasure. I felt good. Didn't think. Loved it.

'Shit, bruv, there's the fool!' Radman pointed out Mozza.

There were three of them. No problems. We both had blades. Cut them and get out of there. Killing never came into my mind. I never thought about it as killing someone. I knew it could happen, but it probably wouldn't. I didn't give a fuck either way. I didn't care if I lived or died. I never expected to live long anyway.

We walked over the road. I led the way. I pulled out a cigarette and went up to Mozza.

'You got a light, cuz?' I asked him.

He didn't know who I was. Mozza was about my age. I didn't know anything more about him than what TJ had said. I didn't even know what he was supposed to have done.

'There you go, mate.' He passed me a light.

I lit it up slowly as he carried on his chat with his pals. He took the light back but I just stood there, smoking. Radman looked ready. I stared at Mozza until one of his mates noticed. Mozza turned around.

'Can I help you, cuz?' he said forcefully.

I launched a sledgehammer punch, missing him by a mile. Wasted.

'What you doing, you fucking prick?' he said.

Radman started fighting with one of his mates. I pulled out my knife and lunged at him. I stabbed him in the arm, then head-butted him. I went in to hit him again, then saw he had a blade. He swung it at me, slicing my hand open like a piece of kebab meat. My hand gushed with blood.

'Let's go!' I screamed at Radman. I could see he had his knife out, too, but I wasn't sure if he'd used it. I didn't care. I was too worried about my hand.

We ran across the road and jumped on our bikes and rode off as fast as we could. We got out of the town centre. My hand was dripping with blood. I was in agony.

'Wait here.' Radman ran into a One Stop. A few seconds later he came out with a load of Special Brew.

'Go!' he screamed.

He obviously hadn't paid. We rode further until we got on to the estate and were well out of the way. We drank two cans each and smoked a load of spliffs. I couldn't feel anything then.

'You need to get to the hospital, bruv. That needs stitches.'

'Nah, fuck that. I'll sleep on it. Be fine.'

'I can see your fucking bone. It's sick!'

'You should have seen the other joker!'

We both laughed and chanted, 'BLUT, BLUT.'

'I'm gonna pop to Lisa's for a bit.' Radman fancied a shag.

'Safe, bruv.' We touched fists.

* * *

It was getting pretty late so I decided to head back to Clear-View. I'd roamed the streets and got through all the drugs I had on me. Even though I was pretty mashed, my hand had started to fucking kill me again.

I rode my bike really slowly. It was dark, with only a few weak street lights, as I went through the field and the park on my way back. I was holding on with only one hand, looking at the other; staring at my mess.

It was cold. Shit. Freezing. There was no one around. You'd get some gangs boozing and getting caned over there, but that night it was fucking Baltic. All I could hear was the 'zzz' noise of my wheels going round and the squeaking of my pedal arms. They needed oiling. Bad. They sounded worse than usual at that time of night, in that field.

As I looked at my hand, all I was thankful for was that it wasn't my drawing hand. It would have driven me mad if it had been.

'CAIN?'

'OH, FUCK.' I fell off my bike. Jumped out of my skin, proper. I didn't expect to see anyone at all.

'Lily, shit! What the fuck you doing here?'

Least of all her.

'I can't stand him; he's such a fucking prick. You get me?'

I didn't have time to answer.

'Sket this and cunt that. I'm sick of that fool.'

'Jog him on then. How many times I got to tell you,

huh? Seriously, what the fuck you doing roaming around a field on your own this late? Crazy bitch, you'll get yourself hurt.'

'I'll be on my way then.' Feisty, very feisty indeed.

I ran after her, 'Whoa, whoa, easy girl. That's not what I'm saying. Girls get themselves raped by not playing it clever. Wouldn't want anything bad to happen to you, ya know.'

She relaxed and smiled. The way she looked at me. Shit.

'So you do care, huh? I came over here cos I knew you'd bike through this way. I wanted to see you.' She moved closer to me. Too close.

'Erm, you got any weed? We can have a smoke, like?' I asked her. Nerves. Bags of them.

'Remember the first time we saw each other? I saw you looking at me.'

'Could do with a fat spliff!' I was doing anything to change the subject.

'You were looking at me doing my clothes up. I saw you. That CUNT stabbed up Ox. But you, I noticed you looking at me.'

I pulled out a fag, 'You got a light?'

'I've always caught you looking at me. And you know what?'

I took a second before answering, 'What's that?'

'I like it a lot.'

She moved in to kiss me but I pulled away. Mashed but I still resisted.

'Nah, Lily, fuck, stop that. TJ is a bad man. Don't need that shit.'

'What, you can't handle that fool? I guess you're not who I thought you were.'

'It's not like that, the boy's a cunt. Hate him.'

'Then be a fucking man. You kissed me a few times, but then nothing. What's up with you, you scared?'

'Fuck that, no!' I said defensively.

'Then prove it, big man?' We stood there in silence.

'Just what I thought. You run around with a knife and get fucked on drugs, but when it comes down to it, you're just a fifteen-year-old kid with no balls. Act like a man but you're fuck all.'

I hadn't even turned fifteen yet. But no one called me that. No one. TJ was a cunt. Fuck him.

'Yeah? Come here . . .' I pulled her into me.

Freezing cold, both high as kites, we did it for the first time. I felt in heaven. I had always wanted her. I couldn't have fucked up more if I'd tried . . .

SYSTEM OF A DOWN

I was sweating like a madman even though the morning frost was everywhere. The Christmas decorations were up all over town. But at half seven in the morning they hadn't been turned on.

I'd not been to sleep. It wasn't just the insomnia that was keeping me awake. I was clucking like a maniac and I needed a hit. Although, even when I'd had a hit I rarely got comfortable enough to sleep.

I was living on the streets. I'd fucked off out of Clear-View. I can't remember if they kicked me out or I left. I was fifteen so I'm pretty sure it wasn't the former. Duty of care and all that bollocks. But they definitely didn't do much to try and find me.

My last few months there hadn't gone well. I had nicked the head's car and burnt the piece of shit out. She got a new one on insurance and I did the fucking same again. She knew it was me and I knew she knew. But she was lacking one fundamental thing: proof. I pushed her over the top one day and she slapped me around the face. Lost her job over it, too. Just like that. They even asked me if I wanted to take criminal proceedings against her. She had done it in front of a load of classmates and another member of staff, so she was bang to rights. Done. Common assault was all it would have been, though. I'd have got hardly any compensation for that, so fuck it.

That's all I was interested in: getting money. Big time. That and fucking Lily whenever I could. If I wasn't getting high, I was fucking her. Or a cocktail of them both.

After I got the head sacked I could see the other teachers hated me even more. Even Pritchard lost it with me – that was like turning a vicar to football hooliganism.

Radman had gone. Joined the Anglian Regiment. Became a soldier for Queen and Country.

'It's three square meals, decent dough, a place to sleep and somewhere to live. You wanna get your head screwed right, bruv. It's shit round here, full of junkies and losers.' His final words were, 'I'll keep in touch, bruv.' It'd been months and not a fucking dicky bird.

He wanted out and who could blame him? I fucking did. I hated it. I hated the world. I didn't have any friends. Some kids were scared of me so they'd be nice out of fear. But I had fuck all. Nothing except strong alcohol, skunk and heroin. Yeah, fifteen and I was on the smack. Big time.

TJ gave me a taste and that was all I needed. It became my life. I was whacked out my tree all the time. And when I wasn't, I was on the rob to fund it. It doesn't come cheap. No. Fucking stuff is evil. Dirt. I couldn't get it from TJ any more. Had to avoid him, considering I was fucking his missus and had been for months. Yeah, she was still his bird. Why? Bitch.

There weren't many boys of my age on the brown. Just a few. I was the youngest I knew. But it was my reality. Most nights I was on the streets. I'd get through them with Special Brew and drugs.

It was weird. I had never really thought that much about Sick Boy after leaving that family. But when I turned fifteen, his spotty, ugly, fucking mug would appear for no reason. He just popped in my mind and when he did I either needed to hit something or get whacked out my mind. Soon enough I was addicted to doing both.

As I stood there that morning, I needed a hit. Badly. Fuck. It's like a hunger that you just can't satisfy. Imagine being thirsty and there being no water. It's something like that. I was in the Sahara and fading fast.

The town centre was still dead. People were in the shops getting ready to open, but everywhere else was quiet. There wasn't much daylight either. Dawn had barely broken, even though it was already half seven. I was in a side alley; waiting.

My breath stained the air as my lungs worked over-time. But still I was sweating. No. Freezing. Both. Clucking. Help.

I'd been waiting for about an hour, but no one had turned up. I was getting desperate.

Bingo! Finally a woman walked up to the cash machine. My heart raced and my mouth filled with saliva as I thought of scoring some smack.

I looked left and right, made sure there was no one around and then started to run towards her. When I was three or four feet away, I pulled out my knife.

'You scream, I'll cut your throat,' I said, as I grabbed her from behind.

'Please don't hurt me!'

'Shut your fucking mouth. Type in your pin number.'

'What?' She was shitting herself.

'Your fucking pin number; type it in.' I looked around – still no one there.

'Please don't hurt me, I've got children . . .' She started to cry.

'Shut up. Do what you're told and fuck all will happen. Balance?'

'Sorry?'

'Listen to me, you cunt.' I roughed her up. 'Show me your fucking balance.'

£3259.87 – for some reason I remember that figure as clear as day.

'I want the lot.'

'I . . . I can't . . .'

'Don't make me cut you, bitch.'

'I have a maximum withdrawal of five hundred.'

Of course. Out of my mind.

'Do it then, don't just stand there.'

She could barely control her shaking hands. I think she was struggling to see through her tears.

She punched in the correct buttons, but it was still taking forever.

'Come, COME ON,' I shouted.

I was looking around, agitated. Hurry. HURRY. The cash dispenser finally opened. I grabbed the money and legged it.

I took a deep breath and knocked on the door. I knew I shouldn't have been there. I had been told NEVER to go there. A well-dressed woman in her thirties answered.

'Er, hello miss, is Robert around please?' I asked in my poshest accent. Yeah, that was really going to work as I stood there with a soaked-through and dirty tracksuit, worn-out trainers and a baseball cap that had seen better days.

'ROBERT?' she shouted, but without taking her eyes off me.

She was disgusted that I was at her door. It was a nice estate. BMW on the drive. Pretty garden. I was not welcome.

'Yes, love?' he shouted back.

'It's for you,' she said, in utter disgust.

He came to the door. His face could barely contain his anger.

'OH, this is Cain, love. He wants a job down the yard.' He gave me an evil look. 'But I told him NEVER to come here.'

'Yeah, sorry about that. Was urgent, need the work, you know.' She wasn't taken in by our charade.

She went back into the house, shaking her head, pissed off. Robert stepped outside, half closing the door. He looked back to make sure his missus was well out of earshot. He grabbed me around the throat.

'What the fuck do you think you're doing coming to my gaff, you horrible little cunt?'

'I'm sorry, Rob, I . . .'

'I should cut your fucking face off for coming here, you cunt. My missus will hit the fucking roof.'

'She's got to be blind if she don't know what you're doing.'

He punched me in the gut, flooring me. True, though. He had a little skip-hire firm, two or three trucks, but the nice car, pretty clothes and the holidays his wife was used to having was courtesy of Rob's sideline in dealing smack and crack.

'Who the fuck do you think you're talking to?'

'Whoa, I'm sorry, I'm sorry. I'm not thinking straight. I need some gear to make me well.' That's how it was – to make me well. Without a hit I was a gibbering wreck.

'You still fucking owe me for the last lot, you sketchy little cunt, so do one. I see you here again, I'll do you.' He wasn't bothered that I was fifteen, that's for sure.

'I got your money. Look, see?' I pulled out the wad I'd robbed and reached up to pass it to him.

Funnily enough, his face changed and he got a little bit friendlier. A little bit.

'Won the lottery? Never mind.' He snatched the cash out of my hand, counting it out. He kept most of it, throwing a few notes on to the floor beside me. He looked around making sure his wife hadn't come back out. One of his neighbours was going to work. He looked over at us – me on the floor with Rob standing next to me. He bent down and helped me up.

'YOU SHOULD TIE YOUR LACES BETTER,' he said loudly, so his neighbour could hear. He wasn't impressed. He got in his car and zoomed off.

'I fucking told you never to come here. Do it again, boy, and I'll do you proper.'

'Sweet, bruv, no problem.'

'I'm NOT your fucking bruv.' He handed me a big bag of heroin and I ran off. It felt like Christmas had come early.

I hadn't looked at the time, but I'd seen a few kids walking to school. I got right under the climbing frame so I was as concealed as I could be. The truth is, you could see me with ease, but in my warped mind I thought I was invisible.

I needed a hit quickly. I got out some tin foil and an empty biro pen and smoked a load of it as quickly as I could. As the dirty, tarry smoke went down, I felt an instant bliss. I felt better even before I smoked it. The thought of it was a relaxant. A reliever. I knew it would be in my system sooner rather than later, so I felt better.

'Urgh, that sick fuck is smoking smack.' One of the kids shouted and pointed.

'Yuk, dirty junkie, that's bear sick!' They all laughed.

'Suck ya mum, you cunts,' I screamed back. They all just laughed and pointed, disgusted by me. I put the gear in my pocket and ran off.

The shop was pretty busy and I was the last in the queue. I felt good. Relaxed. Fucked. High. Low. But I wanted a drink, too.

I had some blackcurrant Chewits, a Kinder Surprise, a Snickers, four bags of McCoy's and a Ginsters sausage roll. Oh, and four litres of White Lightning, the strongest cider I could find.

The queue was going down nicely. I just wanted to pay and get out of there.

'We don't serve until eleven a.m.' He was rude.

'Nah, bruv. I want this now, yeah?' I started counting out the money.

'I'm not selling you anything. You're not even old enough.'

'Yeah, I am. I'm nineteen,' I said, all cocky.

'My arse. On yer bike.' He was an old geezer who obviously hated the youth.

I looked around – there was no one behind me. He had

a small selection of birthday cards beside him on a metal stand.

'Fuck you, bruv!' I grabbed it and smashed it into his face and ran off.

I didn't even hear him move, let alone bother to chase me.

My hands were killing me. Two two-litre bottles of cider were difficult to carry without a bag. Once I was well away from the newsagent's, I stopped and filled my socks and pockets with the sweets and crisps.

I smashed the sausage roll straight down my neck, though. I was hungry. Always fucking hungry. The whole time I wanted food – I never seemed to get enough. They say drugs are a food suppressant – yeah, they are for most. But not for me. I was so malnourished and underfed, I was always hungry. My body needed calories. It craved them.

I ended up back on Robert's estate, funnily enough. Nice. Suburbia. The last person I wanted to see was him, though. But, low and behold, he drove past in his swanky M3 with his stuck-up wife beside him. If looks could kill . . . He couldn't believe I was back there. His estate. But I wasn't there to see him.

I turned right into a lovely little cul-de-sac. Only four or five big houses were down there. Probably the best gaffs on the estate. I hid behind a couple of huge fir trees at the front of the first house. I was going to the house down the end, but I just needed to make sure there were no cars outside.

I looked. I looked again. All clear. Perfect. I wandered down the road, my hands felt like they were going to drop off. I pushed the doorbell with my nose.

'Fucking hell, Cain, why you carrying that shit in the open? The neighbours will tell my parents.' Lily wasn't amused.

'When I robbed the place, I couldn't ask for a bag, innit.' She looked left and right, making sure no one was looking and then pulled me in. She smiled. She got off on all my bad stuff. She loved it.

Daddy thought his girl was prim and proper – she was doing her A-levels, when she bothered to go and wasn't seeing me or TJ. But it didn't really matter if she went or not. The girl was blessed. The Midas touch. Believe. Even though she knocked around with bad boys, she still got good grades at school.

She loved a bad boy, though. Got turned on by it. Upper-class girl, sorted family, big house. And she was fit. Damn! But she got hooked on TJ in the early days. And then me. And it had been that way for some time. Although it was him, then me. It was actually him AND me.

She liked the fact that she was with two boys who, let's face it, were fucking horrible. And who were former friends. He wanted to rule me like every other one of his mugs. But I wasn't having it. I had distanced myself from him and had started to go out robbing on my own terms and for what I wanted. I didn't like the fool. He was crazy and unpredictable. Plus I loved Lily. Yeah, loved. He treated her like dog shit. I think she would have left him if I'd have fronted him like John Wayne and 'saved' her. Fuck that, though. I was handy and nasty but I didn't need that problem. She LOVED the problem. Big time. Still, I kept seeing her because I was addicted to her, as much as I was addicted to the drugs and booze.

She grabbed me and kissed me passionately.

'Fucking hell, boy, you stink to high heaven.'

'The fuck do you expect, living on the streets? I ain't got a Jacuzzi and power shower like you.'

'Get your clothes off. I'll wash and dry them while you're here.'

I stripped down to my bare arse.

'Go jump in the shower.'

I knew where it was. This was regular practice for me.

A big shower head up top and jets that blasted away at my body. Fuck, it felt good. Believe. CK shower gel and some poncy posh shampoo.

The base of the shower turned literally black from the filth that fell from my body. I was black with dirt. I had a horrible bum-fluff beard, too, and an overgrown, shaggy barnet.

I got out of the shower and dried myself down. I knew where her dad kept his electric razor – some imported, super-duper, 'cut-your-face-off' machine. I ran it over my face, making it as soft as a baby's bum.

Once I put it back and shut the mirror, I saw that I actually looked my age. My washed, frizzy hair and my soft skin. But I had glassy eyes and a grey complexion from being worn out and living hard. I didn't stare for long. Too much reflection, too much thought, can kill a man. That's how I felt.

I sprayed my body with her dad's expensive deodorant, slapped on some aftershave and put on his comfortable and fluffy robe.

As I went downstairs, I could hear the music pumping out loud. I walked into the kitchen and Lily had poured two pints of my cider – hers was half drunk, mine on the side. She had a load of cocaine racked out in lines on the breakfast bar. The music was fucking loud. The speakers were in the ceiling and they were screaming. She was dancing around, drinking her cider. She bent down and snorted a line. If daddy could see you now. I thought it was funny when I found out she was a silver-spoon child. You'd never have guessed it in a million years.

She saw me walk in. 'You fucking used my dad's shaver again? I fucking told you not to, he'll notice.'

I just rubbed my clean-cut chin and smiled. I grabbed my cider and downed half of it in one go.

Suddenly, I remembered, 'FUCK! Lily, I had a load of brown, my blade and some money in . . .'

'It's over there.' She pointed to it.

Thank fuck. I thought she'd put my heroin and money through the washing machine. That was all I needed. I did a couple of lines of Charlie and Lily poured a couple of shots of her dad's expensive, flavoured vodka.

It wasn't long before we'd polished off the bottle, all my

cider and her Charlie. I felt wired to fuck. Lily just seemed pissed off we didn't have any more.

'My clothes dry yet?' We both went over to the dryer, barely able to walk.

She got them out. 'There you go.' She had that 'look' in her eyes.

All she had to do was look at me in a particular way and I was aroused like a maniac. She slowly undid my robe. I pulled at her clothes and we had mad sex, right there. High, drunk and unprotected sex.

'Shall we have a pipe?' she asked, no sooner than we'd finished.

She was a mentalist. She would drink shit loads and take loads of drugs all the time but somehow she wasn't an addict. I guess that's wrong. She probably was addicted in her own way, but not like me. She could go without. Return to her normal life and be the posh man's daughter. Me, I couldn't get through any waking day without being smashed out of my fucking nut.

We went outside and smoked a load of smack. Easy. Felt good. I was totally zonked. Fucked. In a haze from the permanent cocktail of chemicals I'd taken. It was like a constant blanket of inebriation.

She became giggly. I was hammered, but still wearing her dad's dressing gown.

'What?' I said, grinning.

'Fucking state of you in Dad's robe, you look like a right tit!'

'Ooh, I'm a connoisseur of heroin, pass me the pipe,

darling!' I said in a mock-gentry accent.

I had another smoke, and then she hit me with it.

'TJ knows about us.'

All blasé like it was fuck all.

'WHAT?'

'TJ. He knows.'

'FUCK.' I couldn't believe it. 'How the hell does he know?'

'I told him.'

She was so calm. As if it meant nothing. She knew it did, though.

'You stupid fucking bitch, what the fuck were you thinking? The cunt will kill me.'

'That's what he said.'

I couldn't believe my ears.

'This is what you've wanted all along, you fucking sket.'

She slapped me around the face.

'Don't you EVER call me that. I get enough of that from him.'

We went quiet.

'Why did you tell him, Lily? Why?'

'Bastard spiked my drink with Rohypnol. I've no clue what he did with me. Afterwards, he goaded me, saying he fucked me in front of his friends while they filmed it. Slag this. Sket that. The normal bollocks. I just couldn't take it any more. So I told him.' She looked upset. Vulnerable. She was a tough girl but for the first time she looked sad and with good fucking reason.

'What did you say?'

'I just told him.'

'I know, but how? What did you say?' I needed to know, I was shitting it, big time.

'That he'd better never touch me again, or you'd kill him. Then he said, "Why would Cain kill me?" And I said because I've been fucking you for ages. And . . . And . . . I love you and you love me.'

Love is not always romantic and rarely comes in all its idealistic glory. But it was there, I guess. Trust. Was she a bad girl? Yeah. Was I bad? You know it.

I put my hands to my head, 'You don't know what you've done.'

'Yeah, I do. He says he's gonna stab you up. Teach you a lesson you won't walk away from.'

'FUCK.'

'You ain't scared are you? Fuck, I thought you loved me?'

'Course I'm not. That fool comes near me, he's got fucking war on his hands. Trust.' I was full of bravado and bullshit. Only way. Kid.

I went inside and got dressed but I was panicking like a madman. I was doing a job of hiding it. I didn't want her to see me scared. My pride was still important, even though I knew what sort of fight I had on my hands.

TJ had a bad reputation for hurting people. There were rumours he'd bumped off a few boys. I think that was shit. Even so, I knew he was capable of it. I'd seen him lose it. Bad, bad man. Fuck.

I got dressed, put my cap on with the hood over the top and got the fuck out of there.

I was bowling through the estate. I'd been searching high and low. As much as I was scared, I knew I had to try and rumble him first. If I didn't, I was well and truly fucked.

I was sipping on some Special Brew and snorting dabs of smack as I wandered around. I'd left my blade back at Lily's. My only protection. In my confusion, I had grabbed my gear and my money, but somehow forgot my weapon. Shit. I was in a bad, bad way.

I couldn't go back, her parents were home. I couldn't go and hide, I'd have looked the coward. The pussy-hole who's scared to fight. Fuck that. Brave man. Stupid boy.

There was a small building site just off from the sea front. I went there looking for something that I could steal to use as a weapon. I didn't know what I was looking for, but I was certain there'd be something there that I could use.

I squeezed in between the temporary gates. Piece of piss. I looked around. It was really dark. All I could see were mounds of stone and sand. No bricks, fuck all. Until I stumbled across a loose wheelbarrow. It had a bucket in it. As I looked closer, I saw a stick inside the bucket that they must have used to mix the cement, or plaster, not sure what, I'm no builder. I picked it up. It wasn't a stick. More like a crowbar. It was metal and heavy. I'd found what I was looking for.

I carried it down the inside of my trouser leg. It was

about two-and-a-half-feet long. I pulled my waist string as tight as I could to keep it from slipping down my leg. It wasn't perfect, so I kept my arm hanging down, holding it tight to my body.

I went looking for him around all the parks and the places I knew that he hung out. I wasn't even subtle about it. I was gobbing off to anyone who'd listen. The drink and drugs hadn't helped. But my attitude and age played a part.

I couldn't find him anywhere. I started to think it was all bullshit and then, 'CAIN.'

I didn't even get the chance to turn around. BANG!

I saw a white flash and I was lying on the ground. TJ was standing in front of me, shaking his hand. He had punched me so hard, I barely knew where I was.

'Fucking pussy-hole, banging my bitch, huh?' He booted me in the guts. Hard. Very fucking hard. I couldn't answer. 'Dirty fucking sket, that's all she is. My spunk bucket, no more than that. Whore.'

I saw three or four others behind him. I couldn't make out their faces. They were his boys, cheering him on. He went to kick me again, but somehow I caught his foot and I swept away his other leg, bringing him to the floor.

I scrambled to my feet, but was still dazed and confused. Punch drunk. Drink and drugs drunk. The others cheered some more. I was about to run but TJ was on his feet. He pulled out his blade.

'You're fucked now, blood. I'm gonna carve you up like a pig.' He was stepping closer. Controlled. Fearless.

The street light glistened off the blade. I knew it was coming for my chest. I wanted to run. My feet were stuck. I should have tried harder to move, then maybe he'd have stabbed me in the back. Fuck. I don't know.

I reached for my weapon, but it had slipped down my leg. Shit. I loosened my jogging bottoms enough to get my hand in. Shit, he was getting closer. Ready to lunge. I was seconds away from being opened up.

I managed to get my hand around the bar. YES. His boys were cheering like madmen. Believe. He was inches away. I still hadn't got the bar out fully. Hurry up! He lunged at me, I dodged. The bar was out – BANG!

A horrible, cracking squelch. Sick. Bad. I didn't just hear the noise, I felt the vibration as I cracked the bar into his head. He let out one yelp and then there was a nerve-shaking corpse on the floor. That quick. He was dead.

'RUN,' shouted one of his crew. They scattered off.

I stared at his body for what felt like hours, but I'm sure it was only a few seconds. I had felt his life disappear the moment I'd connected.

I dropped the weapon and ran for my life.

GAS PANIC

I looked around the room, I didn't have a fucking clue what was going on. Everyone stared at me. There were people buzzing around the court trying to look busy, but I knew better. Nosy bastards.

Everyone was looking at pieces of paper and files, whispering to someone near them, looking at me and then whispering again. It was doing my fucking nut. None of it made any sense to me.

I had a social worker beside me, who kept nodding at me, with a stupid, caring smile slapped on her face, and mouthing, 'You OK?' every two minutes. I just wanted to scream.

I'd not had a hit for nearly twenty-four hours. I was

shaking like a dog. No drink or drugs. I couldn't sit still. The courtroom seemed to close in on me. Every now and then I'd jump up and try to walk off. The social worker and my brief would pull me back down. The fat security geezers were ready to pounce. I'm sure they were hoping my people would lose their grip so they could jump me. Come on, blood, I'll fuck you up, too.

All night I'd been in a police cell. All night without so much as a cup of water. But my arrest hadn't exactly been plain sailing. Believe.

After TJ had . . . After the fight, I legged it proper. Ran like the wind, man. Everyone else scarpered, too. But somehow, in my fucked-up brain, I thought it'd be cool and no one would catch up with me. Mashed, totally mashed. So I went over to the field, the one where I'd hang out, the one where Lily and I first . . .

There were a few boys there getting stoned and hanging around. Normal. I went over to them to score some gear. All they had was skunk and cider.

'Blood, I beg you for some,' I said.

They all knew who I was. I sometimes had trouble remembering my own name, let alone anyone else's but I recognised them. They were scared. I could sense it. I was the homeless junkie. Bad man. Dirty. No one likes a loose cannon.

Reluctantly they gave me a can and a spliff. Keep me quiet, stop me from kicking off. I downed the can and was passed another. There wasn't much said. I smoked the spliff as they watched.

'Is he dead?' one of them asked. He was only a kid. Yeah, I was fifteen but this boy must have been about twelve.

'Shut up, Stevie.' His older brother gave him a dig in the ribs.

It went silent as they looked on. I think they all wanted an answer. I was shaking like a leaf. I wanted to get even more smashed. Anything to take the crunching squelch away from me. It was being played over and over in my mind, like a broken DVD stuck on repeat. I could hear it, feel it, see it. It was bad, man. Believe.

'Yeah, the cunt is dead and good fucking riddance.' Full of bravado and bullshit. Still acting the big man.

'What was it like?' The innocence of that young lad – he asked me things the others dared not.

'It felt like I was the crusader and he was the dog that needed putting down.' Who the hell did I think I was?

Some pissed-up sket came rolling over. 'Yuk, you got blood all over your hoodie. That's sick.'

I looked down. I'd not even noticed. There wasn't a lot, just some blobs here and there. But it was thick, like treacle. Blood from deep inside that should never see the light of day.

The familiar sound of police sirens roared. But these were close. Coming closer. The Old Bill sometimes drove on to the field with their lights off and switched on the full beams and the sirens as they got close. They knew most of the kids would be out of their nut, so they wouldn't have much chance of running if they did it covertly. Any sober person would have heard the car, if not seen it, before it had got close but when you've got a bunch of teenagers getting pissed and wired, they'll hear fuck all.

There weren't any shouts, everyone just ran in their own direction. I simply walked off, sipping on my can of cider. Rebel without a cause. Wanker with no idea.

The feds jumped out of the squad car and came running. I looked around but didn't run. For some reason, and God only knows why, I thought they must have been after someone else. They were running straight for me but still it didn't sink in. There were two of them, both in their early twenties.

'Cain Thomas?' one of them said to me.

'Nah, bruv, he ran the other way.' I didn't give a fuck. I was cool as ice. Just walking and sipping.

'Whoa, whoa,' one of them said as he got in front of me, placing his hand on my chest and slowing me down. 'Cain, don't make this difficult.' He knew me, then.

'Blood, get your FUCKING HANDS off me.' I shoved his hand off my chest.

As I did, I saw him clock the blood on my top. There for everyone to see, like a Damien Hirst exhibition. Both the plods looked at each other, then back at me.

'Where have you been this evening, Cain?'

'Mind your own fucking business.' Gob-shite.

'TJ has just been found dead. So I'll ask you again, where have you been this evening?'

'Round some sket's house, innit.' How inventive.

'What's her name and where does she live? How did you get that blood on your top?' He was edging closer. There was only going to be one outcome. He knew it. I knew it.

'What you need to know that for? You not getting any at home, you fat prick?' I laughed at myself.

'Jokes are over, Cain Thomas. I'm arresting you on suspicion of murder . . .'

Bang! I smashed him around the face with my can. The can was pretty full, which added to the weight and impact of my punch. I cut his eyebrow as I connected.

'ARRGGHH!' I didn't have time to revel in my handiwork. The other copper had taken out his baton and whacked me straight across my calves. I dropped to the floor like a ton of bricks. I wouldn't say they totally battered me. I wouldn't say that. But, yeah, they were rough. I was bruised, I was hurt. But I didn't go quietly. Kicked up a fuss the whole way. Believe. They didn't take any prisoners, metaphorically speaking, when they wrapped me up and cuffed me. No, no. But, considering what I'd done, I'd say I got off pretty lightly.

Once I was back at the nick, they made it very difficult for me to see anybody who was there for my 'welfare'. Being a minor and all that, that should have been my entitlement. But I didn't see anyone. I'm not saying the Old Bill made it hard, maybe no one bothered to turn up. I don't know. But I saw no one until twenty-four hours later in the magistrates' court. One thing I do hold them responsible for is not giving me any food or water, or letting me see a doctor. I was coming down off drugs and booze – an addict. But I got nothing. Perhaps that was their retribution. Fuck knows.

The courtroom stank like a headmaster's office. I was freezing. I'd been given a prison tracksuit. They had to take my clothes for evidence. The silly suit the coppers gave me wouldn't have fit a baby.

No sooner did I feel freezing, though, than I was then dripping with sweat. Clucking, man, big time. All the social worker managed to get me was some paracetamol. Poxy paracetamol. I needed to see a doctor or a drugs counsellor. I needed something. I had more than a fucking headache. I was tripping out my skull. I could barely understand what was happening.

The people at the top table were listening to the prosecution read out details of my past and who I was. They spoke about me as if I wasn't there. That killed me.

'At eight years old he attacked the biological son of his foster carer with a knife.'

I couldn't believe they knew that. No police involvement, nothing. No questioning. Fuck all. I was simply shipped to another residence. But on my record it stayed. Everywhere I went, it was there. That dirty, raping piece of shit got away scot free. Fuck. FUCK.

A speccy bitch carried on reading out a list of my bad attributes. The list was long. Believe. No angel. I know that. But, still, it didn't make it any easier to hear.

'What's happening now?' I said loudly to Emma, my social worker.

'Shhh, the magistrates are going to decide what is going to happen next,' she whispered.

'He was going to do me, end of. It was him or me. That fool deserved it.' My words echoed around the room causing Emma to look on in embarrassment. My brief gave me a stern look. 'WHAT?' I said, aggressively.

'He's on your side, Cain. Please, just for a second, let's wait and listen.' Emma didn't seem to lose her cool.

I couldn't sit still, though. I felt like I had bugs running around my body, just under my skin. I scratched myself. Pulled at my clothing. Shook my leg, went to stand up, then sat down. I looked at the clock, the second hand was vibrating through me. I couldn't stop looking at that clock. It was killing me. Stop. STOP. The eyes of everyone staring, the tunnel vision, my mouth dry, headache, freezing body, sweaty palms, men walking, officials speaking, my body – fuck, it itched. The voices screamed. The echoes of TJ – the cracking, the blood. What if I was him? What if Lily . . . ? Fuck, Lily, where was she? Was she OK? Did she love me? Would I see her again? TJ. How did it happen? The feeling of his life slipping out of him. My mind wouldn't stop, it was screaming like fuck, killing me. Please. Stop. Enough. ENOUGH . . .

'ENOUGH. FUCK. I'VE DONE NOTHING,' I screamed, for everyone to hear.

'Sit down, young man,' one of the officials said. I didn't know who or what he was.

'Come on, Cain, sit with me for just a minute.' Emma was very calming.

In a jittery ball of mess, I sat down. Again. I started to bite my fingers. I had no nails left. Just scabby, dirty, hard skin. The ticking of the clock was still getting to me. The tunnel vision. I was freaking out. Freaking like a mental case.

'I see no alternative than to remand Cain Thomas into custody, pending further investigation.'

Just like that. Bang. He wanted me off to prison without passing go.

'What does that mean?' I asked Emma.

'They are taking you to a training centre while they investigate further.'

'You mean prison! They're taking me to fucking prison. Nah, the geezer was going to do me!'

'A training centre is for young offenders . . .'

'Fuck that, it's prison.' I looked to the magistrates, 'What the fuck would you have done, you stupid cunts?'

The security meatheads were coming for me.

'Come on, Cain, let's go downstairs,' Emma tried to reason with me.

'Nah, fuck that, I ain't going anywhere.'

'Right, son, let's go.' He was a big, fat skinhead.

'I ain't your fucking son, FUCK off.'

He grabbed hold of me with his partner. I tried to head-butt him but to no avail. They were too big and too strong. I struggled and fought with everything I had – kicking, screaming and swearing the whole time. They picked me up off my feet and carried me out of the room. I was over six feet tall. I was a lump, so that was no mean feat.

As we got to the stairs and out of sight, the bullies got more heavy handed.

'Shut your dirty mouth, you little cunt,' one of them screamed as he punched me in the stomach.

'Me and you, you cunt. Come on, blood, let's have it.' You should know when you're defeated but it's something I never knew. I started to kick and struggle like a maniac. I screamed so loud, I went utterly mental. I managed to kick myself out of their hold and break free.

We were on the stairs when he let go and I came crashing down. They reacted by trying to wrap me up, but I tore into them. I can't remember what connected, but I definitely didn't make it easy for them to get me to the cells under the court.

Another screw undid the door and the first two threw me inside. The door slammed. I kicked the shit out of it as I screamed my head off.

I sat in the corner shivering like mad. I was seriously cold. The inside of the cell was dirty, brown stone, with a fixed unit to sit or try and lay on. It wasn't brown paint but brown from dirt. Dirt and violence. I could feel the ferocity that had gone on inside that room before me. It was a scary place.

I didn't feel alone. It was like the walls were watching me. Believe. It was bad, man. Shit. I guess half of it was a sense of the violence the room had seen, the other half was my drug-addled mind. All mixed up with the fear of going to prison. The fear of being behind bars. That's tough for any man. Or child.

I wasn't bothered about being on my own. That was normal to me. It's something I'd become accustomed to. A life without a family was usual for me. I was used to fighting and fending for myself. Not that I didn't crave normality. Or what most would consider a normal life. Normal is the wrong word. A horrible word. But prison, locked up, liberty taken. Nah, blood. Bad shit.

The door of my cell opened, which made me jump out of my skin. I tried to get deeper into a corner, which was impossible. Emma walked in.

'Here, I've got you some food.' She had a cheese roll, a bag of Monster Munch and a Pepsi Max.

They don't give food out at the court, so Emma must have gone to buy it for me. That wouldn't normally be allowed, but since I was a minor. Some perks.

I tore open the roll and scoffed it down in a few seconds flat. Clucking or not – starving. Always starving. Pickled onion crisps. Lush. The Pepsi softened my cardboard tongue. It tasted good. Divine.

'How you feeling?' she asked.

'What do you think?' I was shivering as I ate.

'Look, they're taking you to HMP and YOI Romwell. It's a decent place . . .'

'The Well? Fuck, they have got it in for me.'

I'd heard some shit about that place. Believe. Heard tales from the fools that ended up there. Big fights. Bad screws. Shit. Emma went silent; she knew she couldn't defend the place.

'First thing is we need to get you some treatment. What have you been taking?'

'For what? Nothing.' I was so used to denying that I was on drugs. It was second nature.

'It's easier if you tell me, then I can make sure you get the help you need.' Like butter wouldn't melt. But I didn't accept help from anyone. 'They will be moving you soon. Make sure you tell them honestly what you've been taking, then they can give you all the help you need.' Fuck, did I need it.

I drank down the last of my Pepsi as Emma collected up my rubbish. 'Right, I must be on my way. I'll come to the prison in a few days to see how you are.' And off she went, just like that.

The sound of the door slamming rattled my bones. It made me jump out of my skin. I started to get the shakes and began freaking out.

The door burst open again. Only a few minutes had passed since Emma had left. In walked a handful of screws.

'On your feet,' the front one said. He wasn't fucking around.

I stood up, but slowly. I wiped the side of my mouth and sucked my gums. It was the last bit of kudos I had.

'Don't suck your fucking gums at me, lad. Let's get that straight for a start.'

'What you gonna do, bruv?'

'I'm not your fucking, bruv. It's Guv. We're transporting you to The Well. You fuck about, I'll be dragging you on to the bus by your bollocks. Understand?'

'I ain't going anywhere . . .' Before I'd even finished – BANG! He grabbed me by the back of my head and dropped me to the floor.

'The fuck you doing? ARGH! Get off me!' I screamed.

'Shut your noise, you had your chance.' They'd been told I was trouble and not to waste time. I comply or I'm dropped.

I heard the stamping of size twelve boots as the other screws dived in to assist.

'Get the FUCK OFF ME!'

They were trying to twist my arms into all sorts of angles.

'STOP FIGHTING,' the lead screw barked.

I felt the full body weight of at least two of them as I was pushed face down. It was crushing my ribs. It felt like they were snapping my spine. I couldn't breathe, I was gasping for air.

It felt like Sick Boy all over again. I felt eight years old. I felt violated. Raped. With every ounce of my strength, I tried to get up.

'ARRGGHH – GET THE FUCK OFF.'

I got to my knees. Two full-grown men on my back, and I got to my knees.

'Get hold of his arms,' one of them cried.

They were on the back foot. Believe.

CRACK! I was back on my front, face down. I was

panting like a lion that'd caught his prey. Only I was the one being savaged.

'You fucking animals,' I shouted. I had tears in my eyes. I didn't know what the fuck was going on. 'Arrgghh,' I cried and my arms were snapped behind my back.

'Easy, fellas, take deep breaths,' ordered the screw who had dropped me. I guess he wanted them to get hold of their adrenalin. Fuck knows. But for a minute or two, we all stayed in the same position, breathing hard like athletes at the end of the race. I heard the rattling and clicking of cuffs. They forced my wrists inside them and locked them shut.

'THE FUCK YOU DOING? FUCK.' I was struggling again. This time it was for a slightly different reason – they'd caught my skin when they were locking them shut.

'STOP FIGHTING.' It was like a fucking script being read from a machine.

'My wrist! FUCK.' I felt the blood starting to drip down.

'Shut up, you big baby. You want to fight like a man, take it like one.'

'YOU CUNT,' I screamed.

I was still lying on the floor, but now my arms were behind my back and cuffed. The screw that dropped me had hold of my head.

'Listen to me now, fella; I'm going to give you clear instructions. If you follow them, there will be no more pain. If you don't, we will carry this shit on all the way there. Do you understand?'

I nodded yes.

'Right, bring your knees to your chest.'

I tried a couple of times but I was fucked. Third time I managed it. One screw had hold of each arm and each shoulder, while another who was giving the order still had my head.

'OK, when I say "UP" I want you to step forward so you're on your feet. Understand?'

'Yes, bruv.'

'Guv, not bruv.'

'Yes, Guv.'

'Ready, UP,' he ordered.

I was on my feet. My body felt battered and crushed. I was shaking and panicking. Shit, I needed a hit. I needed a drink. Fuck, I was a mess. Big time.

I was still in a bent-over position but at least I was on my feet.

'Right, lad, I'm going to let you stand up. You fuck about again, I'll be carrying you on to the bus. Get it?'

'Sweet.'

He let me up and for the first time I saw how many of them were there. I had a screw on each arm, the boss man in front of me and two others squeezed in behind for good measure. Serious.

They walked me out of the cell, slowly and controlled. My guts were twisting and turning. The acid had dived on the food I'd just eaten and totally destroyed it. I wanted more food and more drugs.

I felt like I didn't exist. Like it was all a dirty dream.

I started to hear laughing. Evil, nasty laughing. I looked

around at the screws behind me, their faces were blank. Then off it went again. Sinister. Sick. The one in front of me wasn't saying anything. Again the laughter.

'Who the fuck is that?' I asked.

The screw in front of me looked confused.

'What?'

'You keep fucking laughing at me,' I said to him angrily.

'No one is saying or doing anything.'

Again, the sound rang round in my head. IN MY HEAD. I couldn't hear anything else, it was driving me insane.

We started to walk down some steps to the open door. I could see daylight coming through. It was the outside. Freedom. That word kept running through my mind as I looked. That and the joker who found me funny. Fuck you.

I turned to look around at all the screws surrounding me, then back at the light at the door. I just wanted to get out. Run. RUN.

'COME ON,' I shouted, as I threw myself forward. The momentum of my body weight saw me and the screw in front crash to the floor just outside the door. Out in the open. So the world could see. The screw was underneath me, and I tried with all my might to head-butt him. I connected once or twice with his chest, doing no damage whatsoever. I looked up to see a handful of people had stopped to watch.

'Help me, please, help me. GIVE ME SMACK,' I screamed.

I was making no sense. Seeing things. Hearing things. I'd never been so scared in all my life. The other screws pulled me off. I was shouting incoherent obscenities, going absolutely fucking mad.

'Get on the van. Move,' I was ordered.

I couldn't put one foot in front of the other. I'd lost the power to walk. It's like I had forgotten how. Coming down off drink and drugs is like nothing else. Evil. It takes control of every part of you.

They lifted me off my feet and carried me into the wagon. It was tight. The walkway and sweatboxes you had to sit in were a squeeze even for the compliant. But when they are putting you in by force, it's near impossible to move.

They opened a cubicle and sat me inside. I felt a sudden rush of exhaustion. Much to their delight. I don't know if it was the situation, the clucking or the fear that caused it. Probably a combination of all three. They took off my cuffs and kicked my legs so I was huddled up, like a sardine in a box. I put my head back and shut my eyes. I drifted off. At last, something that resembled peace.

My head flung forward with enough force to wake me. I looked out the window. It was pitch black.

I had no idea how long I'd been travelling, but I guess it was for many, many miles. It wasn't dusk; night had completely fallen. I had no idea where The Well was, but I'd heard it was in the arse end of the planet. They weren't wrong.

81

For a few short seconds after I woke, I felt normal. Just for a few seconds. And then the hunger set in. The craving for a hit. The dirty laughing started up. I put my hands to my ears, but that couldn't stop it. Believe. It was so loud it was crucifying me.

I saw some lights in the distance, up on a hill. Other than that, there was nothing. We were in the middle of nowhere. We were driving slowly. Very slowly. We pulled into a car park that only had a few cars in it. I had no idea what the time was but, judging from the car park, it had to be close to the middle of the night.

We came to a stop. I saw the sign lit up in the night, 'HMP and YOI ROMWELL'. I had arrived. I rocked back and forth, feeling uncomfortable in my own skin.

A pair of huge gates opened and we drove in, stopping in a vast, shed-like, sterile area. I noticed the driver get out. One of the screws from the prison walked around the van with him. It looked like a security procedure. All it did was add to my paranoia. I was convinced they were plotting to kill me. I was being driven to my execution. Game over. All the bad things I'd done had caught up on me.

I saw Sick Boy. Then I saw the blood after I'd stabbed him. Like mug shots, every person I'd ever hurt flashed before me. TJ last. I was scared. Shit scared. I couldn't stop shaking. I tried to stand up, but couldn't. No room. Trapped. I needed something to calm me. I needed drugs. I had to have them. I couldn't cope.

The engine started up again and we went through the

next gate. I couldn't see much out of the window. I noticed the silhouette of three or four huge buildings and a dirty, great, big perimeter fence. We were driving close to that on the inside.

The barbed wire freaked me out. I felt like I was dying. Fifteen and dying. The van came to a halt and I heard the door to the back cab being opened. That's when I realised I'd not heard any other voices. The other cons who had been in the van must have been dropped off somewhere else. I was alone.

The key went into my sweatbox and then it was opened.

'No, no, it's not my time, not my time,' I kept on repeating.

'Come on, Thomas, no fucking around now. It's late. I've had enough of playing silly buggers with you.'

He went to grab my arm but I snatched it away.

'It's not my time, not my time.'

He grabbed me by the head and dragged me out. I didn't really fight that much, just begged to be left alone.

He got me outside the van and I could see my breath on the air. I carried on mumbling to myself. I saw three screws in prison uniforms – black trousers and polo T-shirts.

'Thomas, come on, lad. Let's have you inside. It's bloody freezing!' That was the first time I met Mr Byrd, an officer in his thirties. 'Come on, lad.'

Fuck that.

I bolted. I must have got about twenty metres before Mr

Byrd rugby-tackled me to the ground, straight on to the concrete. The cut on my wrist from the cuffs started bleeding again.

'That's enough of that crap, kidder. Let's get you inside.' He tried to make light of it.

The other two screws came over and started to bend me up.

'Come on then!' I barked. I felt ready to fight again. The manic depressive, crazy switch inside me had been clicked. My ticking time bomb was ready to go off. I cracked one of them in the jaw. Huge mistake. They got stuck into me. Big time. Believe. My head was bounced off the floor, my ribs were battered. They kicked the shit out of me.

I remember being dragged past the van. My feet didn't touch the floor and my head was used to open up the door into the building. I went through reception and on to the First Night Wing, which also doubled up as their Seg.

They didn't fuck around; they took me straight to the strip cell, which had fuck all in it except a nailed-down bed.

'This is where we house the shit bags. You will learn, Thomas. Believe me, you will learn.' Mr Byrd had tried the nice approach – but he now found this more suitable.

When you enter a jail, there is usually a strip procedure to follow and ID cards to be issued and stuff. Not always when it's late at night, though. And definitely not when there's some young madman, who's assaulted everyone he could get his hands on since being in the courtroom.

The cell door was opened and I was thrown in. I hit the floor hard. BANG! The door slammed behind me. It was a terrifying noise that stains your eardrums. It was a noise that I was going to have to get used to . . .

MENACE TO SOCIETY
(TRAINEE BIG MAN)

finished my Coco Pops and drank my tea. I felt clear headed. I'd been on an even keel for a while. They had pumped me full of shit as part of my detox plan. Fuck knows what it was but it totally zonked me out. Made it easier. Believe. Emma had made sure I got what I needed to make me better. Well, not better, but sober and able to get through the day in a relatively painless way.

The hallucinations stopped after a few days. They were vivid as fuck. Real. I'd never known anything like it. I was starting to feel strong. Like I was in better control. This prison shit didn't seem too bad. Saying that, I'd not been on a normal Unit with other lads yet. I'd been kept on Seg. I was a mental case, or so they saw it. I was one of the worst drink and drug cases The Well had ever seen. And I was violent with it. Bad. Didn't give a fuck and the more comfortable I got, the happier to swing a fist I became. I was big noise around the jail. All the kids had heard about the nutcase who had turned up smacked out of his tree. The naughty boys who got placed on report would have to attend the Seg for their adjudication. And when they did, some of them would come to my cell door to speak to me. They'd tell me about my status around the place and I loved it. It made me feel that I had a reputation to uphold. That I had to prove to them I was who they thought I was. Big man.

As I finished my tea, I went to the cell door to check there were no screws on the landing. I looked out the spyhole. I couldn't see anyone but I couldn't get a clear view of the whole landing. I put my ear to the door. I was satisfied that I had a bit of time. I put my cereal bowl, pens, pencils and magazines on to the floor, carefully and quietly. They usually sat on top of a little wooden table. I'd been moved out of the strip cell into one that had a few luxuries. Well, I wouldn't exactly call them that but they were gearing me up to put me on normal location. I had other plans.

I heard a door slam, which made me freeze for a few seconds and stare at the door. I waited. I waited a bit more.

The coast was clear. I broke off one of the table legs but, like a clumsy fool, I dropped it. It made a loud noise as it fell.

'Fuck!' I said, quietly.

I heard footsteps on the landing. A screw was coming to check on me. The noise. FUCK. They were drawing closer by the second. I picked up the loose leg and tried to balance it in its former position under the table. Every time I let go of it, the leg started to fall. It was like playing an odd game of Jenga. Shit, the steps were getting closer. I grabbed my chair and somehow managed to wedge that next to the leg, holding it in place. I heard the rattling of keys entering my cell door. I composed myself, running my fingers through my hair. I stared at the leg, balancing in position, praying that it wouldn't fall.

'You all right, Thomas?' Mr Byrd asked.

I looked at him and down at the leg. He hadn't noticed.

'Yeah, sweet, Guv. Tripped and fell, that's all.'

I looked him in the eyes. Stay calm, stay calm. He stared at me, checking to see my reaction.

'OK, mate, take it easy,' he said, smiling before he walked off.

Thank fuck. Thought I was busted before I'd even started. I picked up the table leg and put it down my trousers. Learned behaviour.

I stood there and waited. I knew I'd be unlocked for morning exercise soon. I had other plans, though. And they involved Mr Bishop. He was a complete cunt. There is no other way to describe him. He was six feet six and a bullying piece of shit. He was a Seg screw, so he was supposed to be firmer, but that bastard took pleasure in inflicting pain. He always went over the top, even when it was a relatively quiet time. He'd bent me up shedloads of times for fuck all reason and the worst thing was, I always felt like I could do nothing about it. He was rude, arrogant and heavy handed. It seemed to me that the other screws thought he was a complete wanker, as well.

I'd decided to fucking do him. How? Play the game to get a few more privileges and then – BAM. Was it premeditated? Hell, yeah. I got familiar with what shifts he worked and waited till the time was right. In a sick way, I thought I'd be doing everyone a favour. Besides, it wouldn't do my rep any harm.

That's all I cared about. All that mattered. I didn't give a fuck about my crime or that I was inside. I just lived for the now. The only time I was self-reflective was when I was freaking out with fear from the detox. Once that pain had gone, I didn't give a flying fuck. Selfish. Begged for forgiveness when the walls were closing in, didn't give anyone a thought when I was in charge of my own faculties.

I heard the footsteps bang against the hard landing floor. Someone was coming to unlock me for exercise. At last.

I looked down on myself, checking the leg was well concealed. Even though it was a fairly thick leg, I'd done a decent job of hiding it. I had butterflies flapping around my guts and sweaty palms. I could taste the salty saliva of adrenalin. The door opened.

'Exercise is up, Tank-Engine.' That's what wanker Bishop called me.

'Thank you, vicar.' Fuck you.

'What did you say, you little cunt?' He stepped towards me, looking for a fight.

'Nothing . . .' I mumbled.

'What was that, I can't hear you?' He put his hand to his ear.

'NOTHING,' I answered more aggressively. I hated him. Believe.

'Nothing, what?' He stepped in closer. I looked at him, he was ready to go.

'Nothing, Guv.' I looked ahead trying not to make eye contact.

'That's what I thought. MOVE,' he said, leaning into me.

I wanted him to walk out first and for me to follow. That would have made it a damn sight easier. Improvisation was the order of the day. I walked out of the cell slowly, contemplating my next move. I held the leg in place with my arm. If you were looking for it, sure, you might have noticed that I was walking funny but if not, then no.

As I got to the landing, I walked past the other cells that had bad boys in them.

'Yes, blood. BLUT, BLUT,' shouted one of them as I walked past. In the Seg we had to take exercise alone.

'Yes, cuz.' I tapped the cell door to acknowledge him.

'Keep your dirty hands to yourself, Thomas, or I'll snap them.' Bishop was like that 24/7. Mrs Bishop must have been a happy woman.

At the end of the landing was an office on the right where the Governor's adjudications happened every morning. All the lads who'd been nicked the day before were brought to the Seg to find out what their punishment would be if they were found guilty. More often than you'd think, people got away with it.

The boys hadn't arrived yet and neither had the Governor. As I got out of the landing, I came to a large, sterile area, which had an office in the middle with glass all the way round, a few little rooms off it and a gate that led outside the Unit. There was more room here. Perfect.

I started to breathe heavily and shake with anticipation. The hairs on my body stood to attention and goose bumps were everywhere. I'd waited for this. I slowed down even more as I slipped my hand into my trousers to get hold of my weapon.

'Get your hands out your pants and speed up, you lazy little bastard.' Little? I'll fucking show you. MUG.

He couldn't see exactly what I was doing. Boys walk around with their hands in their pants – it's a done thing. Some screws say stuff about it, others say nothing. Bishop said stuff about everything.

There were a few screws in the office, drinking tea and scratching their arses. This was it. I was going for it. I started to pull the leg out as fast as I could. I saw Mr Byrd looking at me through the glass. Fuck. He saw the weapon.

'PETE,' he shouted through the glass, 'HE'S GOT A WEAPON.'

91

No turning back now. I pulled it out like a fucking lightsaber. I swung around with everything I had – all the might in the world hoping to connect with him. He ducked as it went past him. But I caught a glimpse of what he was made of. Nothing. The eyes don't lie. He was scared. All those times he'd beaten up kids for fuck-all reason, they were coming back to haunt him. Don't think I had an honourable cause for doing it. No. Sure, I hated him and he deserved to be slapped into line, but not by me. I was doing it to show how hard I was. Yeah, how hard.

He turned on his heels and legged it.

'COME ON, YOU PUSSY-HOLE,' I screamed.

'Leave it, CAIN. LEAVE IT.' Always Cain when they're scared.

He ran straight for the Governor's adjudication room. He dived in and slammed the door behind him. The office was a converted cell and it still had a cell door, so the minute it shut, it locked. He was that much of a fucking coward, he locked himself in a room to get away from me. If he had been the man he pretended to be, he'd have stood his ground. But the minute someone stood up to him, his bollocks shrank and his confidence evaporated.

I whacked the door for good measure.

'YOU FUCKING COWARD. YOU FUCKING BATTY BOY. COME ON.'

All the boys in their cells started kicking their doors screaming a chorus of, 'BLUT, BLUT.'

I walked back into the sterile area; all the screws were

huddled in the office. I thought it was brilliant; they were all scared of me. That's what I thought. But the reality was, if someone has a weapon, screws are trained to retreat. It doesn't always work that way and it showed how much they thought of Bishop. They all watched on to see what I was going to do.

'Come on, you screw cunt. One by one I'll take the fucking lot of you.' None of them spoke, they just watched. They wanted a show. I'd give them one.

I started to whack the glass that surrounded the office. BANG, BANG!

'COME ON.'

I hit it over and over and over again. It was reinforced glass – it didn't shatter. I kept hitting it, like a boy possessed. Eventually it started to crack.

There were one or two female officers in the office. They looked scared and were being comforted. The more fearful they got, the more my dick grew. It gave me power. Relevance.

I got to work on cracking every single piece of glass until I was fucking knackered. I dropped the leg to the floor, panting like mad.

'You finished?' Mr Byrd said through the glass.

I had finished. I'd made my point. I'd put the shits up that wanker and made enough noise to ensure the rest of the nick heard about it. I looked back at Mr Byrd.

'Yes, Boss. I'm done.'

'Kick your weapon over there,' he ordered. I did. 'You gonna behave if I come out?'

'Yes, Guv,' I could barely speak I was so out of breath.

He came out and walked up to me. I got in a defensive stance. I thought he was going to try and bend me up.

'Whoa, Cain. I ain't doing fuck all.' He put his hands up to show he was being non-aggressive.

He stopped right in front of me and had a friendly look on his face. Almost brotherly. He didn't ask what I'd been trying to do. He knew.

'Let's get you to the strip cell, lad.'

I knew I was going to be nicked and would have to be dealt with but I had a real sense of achievement. When I walked past the Governor's room, I pissed myself because I saw Bishop kicking the door and shouting, 'Let me out!' I swear I heard Mr Byrd laugh as well.

Safe to say, I'd well and truly found my feet. I felt tough. I felt unstoppable. The big man. Yeah. No one would dare take me. I had no idea how long I was going to stay in that place – there wasn't even a date set for trial. Why I was there didn't even cross my mind. And, until it did, there was going to be some fucking havoc.

THE SPIDERS FROM MARS

I put all my stuff into the huge, clear plastic bag I was given. I didn't really have that much – my prison clothes, some paper and a few magazines.

I was getting ready to move from the Seg over to normal location. I'd been in The Well for a couple of months and I'd not been on normal location yet. Madness. The detox had taken a while, though, and it had caused me to have sporadic periods of violence. The detox and Bishop wanting a tear up every five minutes, that is.

I didn't get as much punishment as you'd think for smashing up the Seg. The Governor just ordered me to have more time in the Seg. An unspecified amount of time – just until I was ready to be relocated on to a normal

Unit. The Governor could easily have shipped me out to another prison as a disciplinary move. That happens when a con is too hard to handle. A drain on resources, as they put it. They fuck the bad apple off to another nick. Governor Myers was a hippy granddad figure, though. He believed in giving people a chance and thought that moving them around did nothing to help. It made the prison's audits look bad if they had to ship people out because of bad behaviour all the time. And Myers was different – he used to take all the shit from other jails. So, The Well pretty much had all of the bastard kids that the other jails didn't want. I worked out pretty early on that was why I'd been sent there.

I put the last of my crap in the bag and sat on my bed. I was nervous about going to the Unit. Not scared, just nervous. I'd not really associated with other cons since I'd got to The Well. The odd pass in the Seg while I was getting my grub, but not much else. I knew I could handle myself and shit, but it was still a turf war out there. I was pretty sure some fool would want to take me down. Be the man who did the crazy boy from the Seg.

I heard the keys enter my cell door. It made me jump. It always made me jump, no matter what time of day it was.

'You ready, son?' Mr Byrd had a smile on his face.

'Guess so, Boss,' I said.

'Good. I got a surprise for you.'

'Yeah? We heading out for a Maccy-D's?'

'It's not that good but you're still a lucky sod. You're

going to be seeing a lot more of me, cos I'm being moved to Mars-Unit with you.' He was grinning from ear to ear.

I half smiled. I was pleased, really. He was the only one screw I got on with. Don't get me wrong, we still had our scraps but, overall, he was pretty decent.

I was heading to Mars-Unit and I guess they thought it best to send Mr Byrd with me, considering all the shit I'd caused while I'd been on the Seg, so they'd have someone on the Unit who could help calm me down when I kicked off. When, not if.

'Fucking hell, Guv, I don't need you to hold my hand, I can manage.'

'We know you can manage, that's the fucking problem!' We both sniggered.

I collected my stuff and followed him out of the cell. I was pleased to be going on to the Unit, even though I was nervous. I was getting sick of being banged up in the Seg. Sick of not being able to associate with people my own age. Plus, there isn't much time out of your cell on the Seg. Bang up, followed by more bang up. I got a bit of sowsh every now and then, but not much. Nothing compared to the normal units. Them boys were out of their cells all the time. Believe. I could do with a bit of that.

I walked down the landing. It was strange, knowing that I wouldn't be sleeping in my cell that night. It was like moving house. Or, better still, being moved to a new home.

I walked out into the sterile area and there were a couple of screws standing outside the office.

'Give them gob over there, Thomas, and you'll see what happens.' Mouthy bastard Bishop.

'Mmm, I've heard the screws stay and fight over there. They don't run away and lock themselves in a cell.'

The other screws burst out laughing.

'You fucking . . .' One of the other screws held him back. Well, he waited for them to hold him back.

I'd worked him out. Fucking coward. And now that he knew I had, the lanky streak of piss never bothered me.

'Good luck, lad,' said the Seg's SO.

'Nice, Guv, I'll do my best.'

Mr Byrd undid the gate and we stepped outside. It was lovely and fresh. The sun was shining and there was dew glistening on the grass opposite. The cool air hit my face as I looked up at the beautiful spring sky.

Even though it was a jail, it was in a picturesque place. It was out in the countryside. You couldn't hear any city noise. Just birds singing and cows mooing. Yeah, cattle just the other side of the fence. The only other noise I could hear were some boys yelling from the windows and a whistle echoing from the gym. Boys were playing basketball or something.

The gym was to my right, which also had a big association room on the side of it. That was used in the evening for boys to play pool and watch TV and stuff. The good boys. Opposite was a big area of grass, with well-kept flowers and shit. That was the centre of the grounds. On the other side of the grass was a building – the Mars and Venus Units. Behind them was an identical building that held Jupiter and Pluto. They tried to categorise the Units so boys with similar crimes were housed together. However, since Myers had opened his arms to every bad motherfucker in the juvenile world, it was proving to be nearly impossible.

To the right of the Units was the education block. Next to that was the main gate. You could pretty much see the whole place from where I was standing. It wasn't very big – not like the big-man jail. It held about two hundred lads.

Mars-Unit had a vicious reputation – boys always fighting and serious incidents always kicking off. Don't get me wrong, the whole place was a fucking war zone but the boys who visited the Seg for adjudication were usually from Mars-Unit.

I walked out on to the grass to head to the Unit.

'Whoa, Thomas, off the grass!' Mr Byrd shouted. 'That's Governor Myers' pride and joy! We walk around it.'

It looked like something from a show home. Proper. We made our way around the grass on the path. There were a few other screws walking the route and Mr Byrd said hello to them.

'What's it like on Mars-Unit then, Guv?' We were getting closer and I could hear some of the boys shouting from their windows. There were only a couple of them – most of the boys were out of their cells, all day long. Education, gym, cell clean, meetings with probation, or the Youth Offending Team as they called it, conduct reports, visits . . . You name it, there was usually a reason for each boy to be out of their cell. The ones left behind the doors were being punished for playing up.

'Play by the rules, it's fine. If not, it ain't easy.' He stopped and turned to face me. 'A lot of trouble goes on in there, I'm not going to lie. A lot of lads just want to cause havoc. It's no walk in the park, that's for sure, and they have all heard about you.' I smiled, pleased with my handiwork. 'It's nothing to smile about. You're a marked man. People want your crown. My advice, keep your fucking head down.'

Here was my induction and the words of warning, 'Keep your head down.' Can't get much clearer than that.

He unlocked the gate to the Unit and we walked in. It was a big space with the showers just off it. I could hear the noise of water and see the steam flooding out. A boy was mopping the floor.

'WHOA, bad man from the Seg. BLUT, BLUT.'

'Knock it off, Apples.' Byrd wasn't in the mood.

That was the first time I saw him. He was a cheeky little fucker. Believe.

Mr Byrd locked the gate just as a boy came down the stairs. 'Guv, I beg you to unlock the showers so I can have one.'

It was Vic. Attitude.

The showers were locked from the outside, so boys couldn't go in there without permission. A control thing. From the inside, though, you could get out. That helped the fat screws who need their rest – they didn't have to get up and unlock every time someone had a shower. There are some lazy fools in the uniform, big time.

'I've just got on here, Taylor, you know the crack. Go and ask your personal officer.'

It was unbelievable how easy it was to roam around the Unit – just ask a passing screw to unlock a door or a gate. Most of them did, for an easy life. Mr Byrd, though, was a man of his word.

'Go on, Guv, unlock it?'

'Taylor, on yer bike, I'm not doing it.'

'Fucking pussy-hole, suck ya mum,' he mumbled under his breath.

'What was that?' Guv stepped towards him. Like a switch, he could turn it on. Nose to nose with Vic, he stood.

'Er, nothing, Guv.' Vic didn't fancy his chances. I smiled to myself. 'The fuck you grinning at, blood, huh?' Vic shouted over Byrd's shoulder.

'Nothing, blood – thought I was, but then it turned out to be nothing. Just like I thought.'

'Who the fuck you calling nothing? I'll bust you up, blood!' he shouted again.

'Leave it alone and fuck off upstairs, Taylor.' Vic tried to step towards me but Mr Byrd pushed him in the chest. 'MOVE,' he said a bit more sternly.

Vic looked at him once more, then at me. He paused for a second before turning on his heels and walking upstairs.

'You'll keep, big man, BLUT, BLUT.' He did his best to scare. Prick.

'Bring it!' I shouted back, with my arms open.

'Welcome to Mars, bruv!' shouted Apples. I smiled at

him. 'He's fucking hench, bruv. I'd steer clear. Bad man. Sick.' Apples offered me his jail wisdom.

'Yeah, and I'm small, blood? I'll bang the fool out.' Vic and I stood at around the same size. Both fucking big for our age.

'You'll do fuck all of the sort, Thomas, or you'll be bounced back to the Seg.' Mr Byrd wasn't fucking around.

Apples and I went quiet.

'I'm Apples.' He offered me his fist to touch.

'Cain, blood. Pleased to meet you.' We touched fists.

Mr Byrd ushered me forward to follow him. He wanted to give me the grand tour. In front of me was a big prison gate and bars. The gate was open for Apples to get on and do his cleaning – or look as though he was cleaning.

'This is the dining and association hall.'

I didn't think it was very big. 'How many cons are on here, Guv?'

'Think it's about forty-five at the minute, but the Unit can hold fifty.'

We turned back and went up some stairs. There were two corridors with cells all the way down each of them.

'This is Landing A and B,' he said.

We went up the next stairs, to the second and top floor, where there were two more landings of cells.

'D-Landing, cell thirty-eight, this is yours.'

Mars-Unit, D-Landing, cell thirty-eight. What an address. Home sweet home. He unlocked the door. The cell wasn't the best. The building didn't look old-fashioned but the cells weren't up to much. But I saw a TV on the side and a radio. It looked like heaven. I'd not watched TV in fucking ages. I was dying for a bit of *The Simpsons*.

'You all right to bang up for a bit, so I can go and put you on the numbers and stuff?' Have a brew and rest, you mean.

'Sweet, Guv.'

'The other lads will be back from education and stuff shortly, and then we'll be doing lunch.'

He shut the door. It was single bang up at The Well for juveniles. I started to unpack my kit – not before putting on the TV, though. Fuck that was exciting. Believe. It was some daytime bullshit. The adverts were what gave me a small sense of normality, though. Very small, mind you. I could have watched hours of them.

I didn't even hear my door unlock, I was stuck in to the TV, like I had never seen it before. It's mad how the small things can mean so much. I hadn't watched much TV before being nicked – not unless it was through a shop window, but still.

'Thomas? THOMAS?'

I looked around.

'It's lunch time, love. Go and get your food – and don't forget to take your plate and mug.' Miss Webber was a really sweet lady. How she became a prison officer was beyond me. She was getting on – I couldn't imagine The Well was a good place to be working at her age.

'Sweet, Miss.' I got up off the bed and grabbed my utensils.

I stepped out on to the landing. Loads of the other boys were already out of their cells, making their way downstairs. They stared at me, big time. They didn't try to hide it.

'That's the guy from the Seg – he fucked up the screws over there,' I heard one of them say.

I stood proud. I stuck my chest out and opened my arms. Carrying carpets. I felt big.

'You got any burn, big man?' asked an Indian fella.

'Nah, bruv, dying for a smoke.'

'There you go, mate.' He gave me some tobacco folded in a piece of paper.

'What's your name?' I asked.

'Raj.'

'I'm . . .'

'Cain Thomas,' he interrupted. 'I've heard all about you.' Oh the flattery. 'You killed some boy, smoked the crack and have been hammering all the screws since you got here.' He knew his stuff.

'You calling me a crack head?' I said aggressively. Calling someone a crack head was offensive. A put down. I didn't mind people knowing I smoked the crack or heroin, though – it made me feel big, proud. I was into drugs more than most other people my age. There were boys inside with addictions but mine was bad. Believe. Fucking bad. I didn't meet anyone else who needed the detox plan I had gone through. In a funny way, it gave me kudos. Gave me an extra edge.

'Nah, blood, I ain't calling you that at all.' He put his hands up; the other boys stopped to watch.

I relaxed a little and offered him a fist.

'Fuck, man! Raj was shook,' shouted one of the boys.

Raj straightened himself out and we walked together.

'What you in for?' I asked.

'Happy slapping. Shit, I left my cutlery in my cell.' He ran back.

I walked on and bumped into Apples.

'How you settling in, Cain?' he asked.

'Yeah, time will tell. What's Raj's story?'

'He's one of Vic's crew—'

'Vic? Who's he?' I interrupted.

'The fella from this morning when you came in. Raj is one of his. But I guess he must be thinking you're gonna whip him, which is why he gave you the burn.'

'What's he in for?'

'Raj? He's in for happy slapping.'

I looked confused, 'That it?'

'He stabbed a tramp to death while his boys filmed it.'

A little worse than I was imagining.

As we were walking down the stairs some of the boys from another landing were coming up with their food. I wasn't really paying much attention to them; I was thinking about the Unit and what was going to be played out. Something obviously needed to be done. And I was sure I wouldn't be the fucking loser.

BANG!

My head hit the wall and I was covered in a plate of

stew. Vic had smashed me in the side of the head with his hot plate of lunch, totally covering me. He landed a couple of big punches, too.

'Laugh at me, you cunt? I RUN THE FUCKING UNIT,' he screamed. The other boys cheered.

I didn't even have a chance to defend myself or retaliate. It happened that fast.

Apples screamed, 'The screws are coming!'

Instead of thinking about what was going to happen, I should have been focussed. Lesson number one.

Vic stopped and stepped back, and all the other boys quietened down.

'What the fuck is going on here?' shouted a Scottish screw, who was out of shape and had a big gob. He was sweating and panting and he'd only run up one flight of stairs.

'I tripped, Guv, spilt my dinner,' Vic said.

Sweaty looked at me and saw the mash and gravy all over my face and head. That combined with the blood and spittle running down the side of my mouth from the punches, and he knew what had gone on but he needed some proof.

'Well?' he asked me.

'Yeah, just like he said,' I replied.

'Taylor, clean this shit up off the floor. Thomas, go clean yourself up then get your lunch. No more fucking around, fellas.'

Vic looked at me and laughed. He'd got one up. Made me look the fool. All the boys standing around could see that. Round one was his. Round one. The cunt better be ready for round two because this fight wasn't going to points.

SCUM

t had fucking great big horns and it looked evil as sin. I'd found it in some Manga comic. It wasn't even in English. But the art teacher had cut-outs and stuff, which we were allowed to copy or use for inspiration.

It was nearing the end of the lesson. I'd worked my nuts off to make it look good. I'd nearly finished the sketch in pencil; I just needed to add some colour. It was the first time I'd done any drawing in ages. It felt good.

All the boys in the class stood around and admired my work – a big devil character in an old warrior suit, brandishing a samurai sword and standing in an attacking stance. It was a fucking brilliant piece of art, and I was pretty pleased with the result.

'Right, fellas, can I have you upstairs please,' the screw who came into the class said. It was the end of the lesson and he wanted us out of the classroom and upstairs, so he could count us out and prepare to move us to our next location. For some of us, that would be back to the Unit, for others it was to another lesson in a different classroom, or on to a visit etc. That's how it was – counted and moved, like a herd of sheep. I found the counting and searching pretty tough at first. I didn't want some perv putting his hands all over my body every time I needed to go somewhere else. That caused a few problems. I would kick off. But soon I realised that it was just one of the rules and, no matter how often I spat my dummy out, it wasn't going to change.

I only had one lesson that morning but I wanted to stay for the second. The only way I could do that was at the teacher's discretion.

'Miss, any chance I can stay here to get this picture done? I'm buzzing off it. Looks the tits.'

'Mmm, OK. Let me check with the officer.' She popped to the classroom door and stuck her head out to call back the screw who'd just come in.

I looked on, clutching my pencil. It was taking longer than I thought. I started biting at it. I really needed to stay. I had to. Come on. COME ON. What the fuck were they chatting about?

Finally.

'That's no problem, Cain. The officer will tell the Unit you're staying here for the next period.' YES!

It was a numbers game – they had to be told. Security and all that shit. All the other boys left the classroom. Sitting at my desk, I could see into the corridor. People were leaving from the other classrooms, too. Each classroom had a big window, they weren't mirrored but it was easier to see out than see in from the corridor. I guess that was to stop boys chatting with those walking past. Perfect.

I watched the last one leave the classrooms. Then there was silence. The block was on two levels. You came in on the ground level, which had two corridors of classrooms, and then you went downstairs to another level of classrooms. The block was on a slight hill.

I knew I had a bit of time. It takes a while for the change around. All that rubbing down and counting. It was a big operation. The whole prison runs from the same timetable and the movements happened the same time every day. The boys would leave one area and walk along to somewhere else on 'the route'. The route was in the open, between buildings, like when I walked from the Seg to Mars.

There were a few screws, here and there, manning the route, with others standing at the entranceways to the other areas. You could pretty much see everyone and everything. The screws had to hurry the boys along the route, to make sure they got to the next place in time. And, yeah, it did kick off sometimes. Badly. Having a load of villain kids walking near each other is a recipe for destruction. Sometimes walking the route was the only time you'd see someone else from another Unit. And if you had beef with that person – BAM! And a lot of the boys didn't give a fuck whether the screws saw or not. The punishments were normally fuck all, if you were sent to Myers, the weed-smoking hippy. Of course, attacking someone out in the open was a last resort. You'd only do that if you couldn't do it on the quiet. Or if you wanted to send out a message not to fuck with you to someone or to another group. No better way than kicking off when you've got an audience on the route.

I'd started putting some red shading on my picture when I heard some lads coming down the stairs. My picture was looking sinister as fuck. By the time I heard them in the corridor, I'd really got into it. Always lose myself in the art. Always.

I looked to see who it was. I lifted up the picture and slid down my seat, to conceal myself a little better. Not that it mattered that much – you couldn't see much through the windows. The boys were chatting and horsing around.

'Let's have you to your classrooms, please,' shouted the screw who manned the landing.

The boys started to filter into the classrooms, mine included.

Fuck, I'd not seen him . . . No sooner had I thought that, than Vic walked past my classroom, heading into the cookery class opposite. Bingo. I let out a sigh of relief. I'd done some digging to find out what his timetable was. I looked back down at my picture. I continued filling in the colour with one eye on the window. Sooner or later I was sure an opportunity would arise.

I didn't hurry the picture at all. I had no intention of finishing it that day. There would be plenty of time. I just needed to do something that would impress the teacher enough to convince her to let me stay to 'finish it'.

I leant back in my chair and stared out the window. Fuck, surely he'd need to go in a minute? It was nearing the end of the lesson. Just as I was about to start colouring again, the door to the cookery class opened – out walked Vic. Shit.

'Miss? MISS?' I shouted, interrupting her talking to one of the other boys.

'What is it, Cain?' She hated being interrupted.

'Can I go for a piss, please?'

'Cain, you know I don't like that kind of talk.'

I tutted, 'Toilet, then. Please, I'm busting.'

'Off you go.'

I got up from my seat and left the classroom. It was normal for boys to go to the toilet during lessons. Anything to break the boredom. I knew Vic would go, sooner or later. I just had to wait, bide my time and keep watch.

Downstairs, where the toilets were, there was one screw on his own who sat at a desk on the landing. He was there in case anyone kicked off. He would jump in and raise the alarm. There was also a screw who sat upstairs, outside the other classrooms. I knew that they might cause a problem. The toilet was about ten metres away from the screw's desk. He should keep it locked and only unlock it when a boy comes out of a classroom and needs to use it. But nine times out of ten, he'd just sit on his arse, with the toilet unlocked, telling the lads to go use it.

I started to get shaky legs and butterflies in my stomach. I knew I had to move fast and that the window of opportunity was only small. As much as the Guv would leave the toilet unlocked, he'd still only let two people in there at once. Luckily, Vic was the only one who'd gone in – I'd been watching.

I moved along the landing quickly. 'Guv, all right to use the bog?'

He just waved his hands to gesture yes. He was sitting back in his chair, with his nut against the wall, barely awake. His eyes were closed. Superb. I walked quickly to the toilets. This was it. Payback time.

I pushed the door ajar and peeked in. He was in one of the cubicles. I sneaked in like a covert fucking mouse. I stood next to the cubicles and waited. He finished his piss. He was about to come out. I was just waiting for the flush . . . I started to shake and tense up, my body filled with adrenalin. I was ready to pounce.

The door unlocked. I clenched my fist and swung the biggest haymaker of my life . . . BANG! I clumped him right in the side of his face. He was a big boy and didn't go down.

'ARRGGHH, WHAT THE FUCK?' he cried.

BANG, BANG! Twice more I thumped his thick fucking head. He fell to one knee.

'You the fucking boy, huh? YOU'RE A CUNT,' I shouted.

I smashed his face with a flurry of blows, until he was crumpled on the floor and then I began to stamp on him. I was kicking the fucking life out the bastard. He tried to cover himself, but I just stamped through it. I knew his head was going to be lumpy as fuck. It had already started to show signs of swelling. I knew he'd be black and blue.

'What handed are you?' I said, breathing heavily and looking around, making sure the lazy pig screw hadn't heard.

'What? Please, I'm fucked.'

I stamped down, 'I said what handed are you?'

'R . . . R . . . Right. Please . . .'

I noticed he still had his cooking apron on. Fucking pussy-hole. I rolled it up and stuffed as much of it in his mouth as I could. I grabbed his right arm and pulled him closer to the cubicles. It wasn't far. He was a tall boy and being laid out flat made it a hell of a lot easier. I put his hand inside the toilet door. It was one of those old-fashioned, heavy doors that went all the way to the floor. You couldn't look over the top or underneath.

'This is the hand that ruled Mars, and the fucking hand that hit me, yeah?'

He was shaking his head, miming no. He tried to pull his hand away, but I was too strong. BANG! I cracked the door hard against his hand and finger. He screamed and yelped, but the apron stifled it.

'It's my fucking Unit now. Understand, PUSSY-HOLE?'

He rolled around on the floor in agony. His hand was shattered. I turned on my heels and got out of there. My heart was racing like crazy. It was doing its best to climb its way out of my chest. I moved fast, with fear and excitement. I walked out of the toilet and on to the landing. The screw was still zzzing on his chair. Believe. I'd fucking done him.

I got back into the classroom and started colouring my picture as if fuck all had happened. Easy as A B C. I felt like the lion. King of the jungle. Nah, I felt like king of the fucking world. There was no stopping me now . . .

CIGARETTES IN HELL

I had more tobacco on me than ever. I could barely carry it. I'd lifted my jumper to form a tray. I had all the boys give me their burn. I was taking the fucking lot. No way was I giving it over to the screws. They wanted it, they would have to come and get it.

Myers had this great idea to make the jail non-smoking. The whole place. He didn't discriminate either. It was the same for the screws and the cons. He believed cigarettes were a cause of bullying for the boys. He wasn't wrong. It was. I used to rob everyone for their burn. Everyone. I never went without and if I didn't get what I wanted, I'd smash someone. Not that it had to happen that much. Raj and Apples always made sure I had enough burn. And sweets. And crisps. Loved my extra food. Loved it.

There weren't any drugs, though. Not really. There would be the odd find, but it was rare. I'd heard stories of bent screws and drugs being everywhere in prison. I'm sure that's the case. In kids' nick, though, the only stuff that ever got through was through the visits. But Myers had cracked down on that. He was doing his best to make the jail a therapeutic, poof's palace. Fuck that!

There'd been a couple of weeks of 'tobacco amnesty'. Gradually, we had all had to give over our burn. It had been knocked off the canteen sheet so we couldn't buy any more. Obviously fags were only allowed to be bought by the over-sixteens legally. The Well housed fifteen- to eighteen-year-olds so some, like me, were under the age. The screws should have checked each time you went to buy it, but they rarely did. It would have caused a kick off. A problem that could easily be avoided by slightly bending the rules.

But Myers had different ideas. He wanted his jail, or trainee bollocks that he called it, to be a flagship establishment. I actually think the old fool thought he could make a difference.

It was the end of evening association and I was heading back to my cell. As I did so, every boy put the last of their burn in my jumper. I was running as fast as I could to get it back to my cell. The screws were asking boys for it as they headed back. I was dodging them and doing my best to get to my cell without being stopped. I got up the stairs and had so much burn I could barely carry it without dropping it.

'FUCK.' A pouch fell on the floor.

I tried to bend down to pick it up. I was struggling to stay on my feet, and then I saw a hand in plaster cast. Vic. He picked up the burn for me and put it in my top. His face was still pretty lumpy but a lot of the swelling had gone down. The dark, heavy bruises were now a yellowy colour. He still looked like he'd had a fucking shoeing, but it wasn't as bad as it had been. I'd broken his hand in two places, along with three fingers. Ouch.

'Sweet, bruv,' I said as he handed it to me.

He looked me in the eye, 'Safe, Cain.' We touched fists.

He didn't say fuck all about the beating. When he finally got to his feet in the toilet that day, he told the screw he'd fallen. They didn't bother looking into it. No witnesses and the boy was saying fuck all. Best left alone, is how they saw it. And that was the end of it. Believe. That's how shit went down. When he got back on the Unit, he was quiet for a few days. Sat back and watched. I was gobby in my victory and had all the boys around me. I was top dog.

Vic was still off-key, though. He let me take the title – well, I forced him to let me take it, but he wouldn't take shit off anyone else. A couple of the boys tried to take liberties with him by making him look a fool. He knocked one boy out with the fucking plaster cast on his hand. Nearly took his fucking head off. As much as I ruined him that day, I knew he was a live wire and not to be underestimated. He was a fucking madman who could change at the drop of a hat. But, for the time being, I was in charge and he was defeated. I got him on side and allowed him into the crew, but he knew his place. Secretly, I knew one day he'd want it back. There were many things that reminded me of TJ about him.

'Thomas, I need all your burn, now!' shouted Sweaty across the landing.

'Whatever, you fat cunt,' I shouted back.

Vic started to laugh.

'What did you say?' I could barely understand him, his Scottish accent was so pure.

'The pies making you deaf as well? You wanna leave them alone and get on the treadmill, bruv.'

'You cheeky bastard.' He started walking towards me with pace and aggression.

I half jogged to my cell. Sweaty had already unlocked all the doors so we could bang ourselves up for the night. I ran in and slammed my door shut. I put all my burn on the windowsill. Shit, I had a lot. I turned around and started jogging on the spot. I was ready for a fight. I knew Sweaty wouldn't leave it. One, he needed to get the burn, the amnesty was over. Two, I made him look like a right twat in front of the other boys. He wouldn't stand for that.

I jogged up and down, the anticipation was killing me. I rolled my sleeves up. That wasn't enough. I whipped my sweater off so I was just wearing my vest. I thought I was Rocky Balboa. I heard the domino bangs of the other cell doors being slammed shut. I breathed heavily. The key went into the door. He even seemed to do that aggressively. It thudded and ripped and the door handle cracked as it turned. The door flung open.

'Who the fuck do you think you're talking to, pal?' he said as he burst in. He kept a few paces of distance between us.

'I ain't your pal, you fucking PIG.' Whoa, I was feeling it.

He started to step closer towards me. 'Give me your burn. I want the lot of it, NOW.' He put a lot more authority in his tone.

'FUCK YOU, it's mine and it's staying with me.'

'You'll do as you're fucking told, shit bag.'

I grabbed my radio, 'Yeah, FUCK YOU.' I threw it at him.

It shattered against his arm as he lifted it to block himself. I booted my chair, which went right for him as well. He ran backwards out the cell, slamming the door shut. Then I went fucking berserk. I smashed my table to bits, along with the TV. I broke everything to smithereens. I put all the debris in a pile by the cell door and started to build a barricade. I threw my mattress on to the pile and all my clothes, linen and everything else I could find. The wardrobe came crashing down as I kicked it with everything I had. I was screaming with aggression as I did so. The bed was made of metal. I stood it up, lengthways, and kicked and bent it until it fell apart. By the time I'd finished, I was fucked. I had one last thing to do, in order to finish my in-cell barricade – I got one of my magazines from the pile, tore a few sheets from it and stuck them over the spy-hole with some Blu-Tack. Obscuring the screws' vision is the final part of a barricade. It's how you protest – a way of being antisocial. For me, it was making the point that I was in control of my own destiny. I wasn't ruled by some muggy prison. I would do as I pleased. I would show them. It made me feel alive.

I went over to the windowsill, sweating and panting. I looked at all the burn sitting there, smiling at me. I chuckled and felt like a fucking hero. I grabbed some Rizla and rolled myself one. Lighter. FUCK. I had all that burn but, in my anger, I'd not left myself with a lighter. I felt destroyed! I looked around at the barricade I'd built and it was a right old mess.

'Cain, CAIN?' I heard someone out the window.

I climbed up on the windowsill and pushed my face towards the small gap of the open window.

'Yes, blood?' I shouted.

I heard a mumble. 'Speak up, blood, I can't hear you.'

'I said, give them fucking shit, cuz, and enjoy the burn.' It was Apples.

'I would but after all that, I ain't got a fucking lighter!'

A load of the other boys started to laugh and cheer. All the boys got by their windows and communicated that way when we were banged up.

'Chew it like a redneck, bruv!' Vic joined in the piss-take.

Everyone laughed. There was a tap at the door.

'Cain? Cain, can you hear me? You OK in there?' I recognised the voice. Miss Webber. I didn't bother to answer. 'Cain, I need to know you're OK?' Silence. 'CAIN?' she yelled.

'Fuck off, you slag,' I shouted back. I could picture her face even as I said it. Putting on a show was more important to me.

'You're OK, then?' she said.

I didn't answer. I jumped off the windowsill and went over to the barricade. Fucking lighter, I needed to find it. I pulled at some of the bed-frame. I struggled to move it, I'd packed it so tight. I was making quite a row.

'What you doing in there, darling?' Darling – bless her.

Again, I said fuck all.

'I think he's barricading,' I heard her whisper to another screw.

'NO SHIT, SHERLOCK,' I shouted.

It was already built but they didn't need to know that. I rummaged around for fucking ages and then, BINGO! There it was; the lighter of love. I ran back to the window and lit the rollie. I sucked on it, like it was the final smoke of my life. As soon as that one was finished, I rolled and smoked another. I chain-smoked so much, my throat felt like sandpaper and my guts curdled. I thought I was going to throw up. Still, I battled on with it. I smoked them because I could. Because I was playing by my rules.

'Cain?' I heard a bump at the door. I didn't recognise the voice.

'He's popped out, can I take a message?'

'Cain, look, we need to sort this out we . . .'

'WHOA, I'll stop you there, fool. WE ain't got to do shit. I'm happy as Larry, thank you very much.'

He went quiet; I could tell he was a bit tongue tied.

'OK, what is it you want?'

'I'll have a Big Mac, a Quarter Pounder with cheese and two double cheeseburgers. Actually, make the Big Mac one a meal.' I was struggling not to laugh, 'With a large Sprite and large fries. Oh, and a Dairy Milk McFlurry!' I burst out laughing. I was pissing myself.

He went quiet for a minute or two. He didn't say a thing.

'We're doing a Big Tasty Special. Can I not interest you in that?' Sharp. Comedy.

I fucking roared and so did he. I liked it. I carried on smoking because I could and choked with every puff.

'Look, Cain, we need to resolve this. So what's the problem?' If they called me Cain all the time, then fine. I'd prefer that. But it was Thomas this and cunt that. But when I had them on the back foot, it was all nicely, nicely.

'THOMAS, YOU PUSSY-HOLE.'

'Whoa, whoa, easy fella. Thomas it is.' He tried to reason with me.

'Fucking Cain when you want something. Cain when you're shitting it. FUCK YOU.' My temper was raging. I was winding myself up.

'OK, OK.' I could hear him lifting up his hands. Defeated.

I looked around the cell; I had totally smashed it to pieces. It was hammered. It looked like a full-scale riot had happened. When the blinkers were shut, I used to go off like a nut nut. I coughed again from the smoke.

'Do you need a doctor or something?' He was getting desperate now.

'No, I'm just enjoying a smoke, innit.'

'Look, Thomas,' at least he was listening, 'whatever the problem is, we can talk about it, and I'm sure if I can't give you what you want exactly, I'll be able to offer you a bloody good compromise.'

'I want to smoke when I want to and do what I want, sweet?'

'Cain . . .'

I interrupted, 'THOMAS, YOU CUNT.'

He quickly interjected, trying to keep the rapport going, 'Thomas, shit, sorry, fella. It's prison, mate. Course there's gonna be rules. That's a fact of life. Shit, there's rules for us who work here, too, and there's nothing I can do about that.'

'Well, if you can't, you're wasting my fucking time – get me someone who can.' I wasn't making it easy.

'It doesn't work like that. If it did, then you wouldn't have been sent here and this place would be pointless.' He was trying.

'It is fucking pointless.'

'I'm sorry to hear you feel like that. If you go with it, you really can turn things around.'

'You in PR, you prick?'

'No,' he answered confused.

'Then stop trying to paint a pretty picture. This is shit,

you're shit and I'm going to smoke when I want. And, while we're talking, why the fuck has that fool banned smoking? I swear he smokes the spliff, anyway!' He didn't, but he always had a hippy air about him. Free love and all that.

'He doesn't smoke "the spliff" as you put it. He happens to think it will be a better place here if it is non-smoking. The health benefits will be amazing for everyone. Plus, those who don't want to smoke won't have to breathe in all the toxins from those who do. Sounds better to me, all round.' Said as if it was read from a pamphlet.

'See, PR. And I bet you're a non-smoker.'

'I am, as it goes.' He was proud.

'BLUT, BLUT,' I hollered, giving myself recognition for working him out.

'So then; how we going to resolve this?'

I was sick of his bullshit talk. 'Look, fuck off, you're giving me the raging hump. We ain't resolving shit. I'm staying in here, you ain't going to invade my privacy by watching, so do one.' I couldn't have made myself clearer.

Again, he went quiet. It was like he had to wait for the cogs to go round in his brain before he could respond.

'Is that your final answer?' And that was the best he could come up with?

'What, you Chris fucking Tarrant, now? Suck ya mum, you fool. Fuck off.'

His voice went a little more hostile. 'Right have it your way, sonny.' I'd got under his skin.

I hopped up on to the windowsill and pushed my face in the gap.

'Apples, you still there?' I shouted.

'Yes, bruv, what's happening?'

'Some fool was chatting shit to me, trying to reason with me and be all gay. Fuck him!' I was showing off. Cock.

Vic piped up, 'Did he give you a final chance?'

I had to think about that for a sec. 'He said, "Have it your way" whatever the fuck that meant. I'm having it my way, BLUT, BLUT,' I cheered.

'BLUT, BLUT, BLUT,' Apples joined in.

I heard a load of boys kicking their cell doors in recognition. Yes, I was the king.

But the king always dies.

'Cain, bruv, they're going to get the Tornado boys.' Tornado boys?

'Who they fuck are they?' It sounded like serious shit.

'A load of screws will get in riot kit, come in there and bend you the fuck up. I'd get prepared if I was you.'

That vibrated around my mind. 'Like to see them try, I've barricaded myself in. They got no chance.' I actually thought I'd be able to stay in there until I was ready to let them in. I never thought they would get in fucking riot kit.

'They get shields and all sorts, blood, believe.' My arse was starting to go.

'Nah, blood, that's big-man jail. They don't use kit like that in here.'

'He's right, bruv,' Apples interjected. 'They fucking do and will, so get yourself ready.'

I put my hands to my head in disbelief. How the fuck? Trying to play the big man. Act the boss. The number one cock. I needed to hand myself over. But that was too easy and the fact that I'd lose face meant it wasn't happening. More bravado and bullshit were required. All the boys had gone quiet, waiting to hear my response.

'FUCK THEM; I'LL TAKE THEM ALL OUT. BELIEVE. BLUT, BLUT,' I screamed.

The Unit went mental. All the boys kicked their doors like fuck. Hammered them. It was deafening. They wanted a show. They wanted to see if the boy of the Unit could handle it. I'd show them. Saving face and being the madman was all that was important to me.

I started pacing up and down my cell. I was nervous. Scared out of my fucking wits. I ran my fingers through my hair. I pulled at my body. I started to sweat. I wasn't hot. No way. It was nerves. My stomach rumbled like crazy. I felt like I was going to shit myself. I chewed away at the hard skin on my fingers, where my nails used to be. I didn't know what to do.

All of a sudden, there was a knock at the door.

'Cain Thomas?'

I didn't answer. SHIT. Maybe they were coming back to chat some more. Surely they don't use all that kit? Nah, not in a young boys' nick.

'WHAT?' I tried to sound as menacing as I could, but my voice croaked. Fear. Did he hear it? He must have.

127

'This is your last chance. I'm giving you a direct order to take away the obstruction from your spy-hole and go and stand at the back of your cell.'

FUCK. IT WAS HAPPENING.

I needed some aggression. More. I needed some hate. Yeah, hate. Hate gets me through, always has. Gives me an inner strength. A reason to fight. Sick Boy. Dirty, raping cunt. I want him dead. I hate him. Vile fuck I could kill him. Dirty fucking bastard. Come on, I'm ready. I'M READY. The thought of him. FUCK, I CAN FIGHT – I WILL FIGHT. I jumped up and down, ready to kill.

'COME ON,' I screamed.

I bounced up and down, I was ready. READY. I didn't hear the door unlock. That threw me straight away. It should have been banging hard against my barricade, but no. The door opened in a split second the other way. Tactical. Fuck, and there they were. I saw a screw with a dirty, great big shield and huge helmet on his head. He had his visor down, which was practically mirrored. I couldn't see his eyes. They were like SAS stormtrooper nutters.

'AND PUSH. AND PUSH,' they shouted in rhythm.

The geezer with the shield was banging down my barricade, supported by two other stormtroopers behind him. I don't know if it was the kit or what, but none of them looked small. Believe. Not one of them. I watched them smash through the barricade with ease. It was crumbling before my very eyes. And I thought that I would come out when I wanted to. Naïve. Stupid. Kid.

I bounced up and down. My mouth had gone dry, my body was shaking uncontrollably. My vision went tunnel. Sound became tinny. SICK BOY. SICK BOY. SICK BOY. I heard the kicking on the other cell doors. They knew what was going down. A battle. A fight. A fucking in-cell riot. The first screw was just getting over the barricade; the other two closely behind. This was it. THIS WAS IT.

'COME ON,' I yelled.

He was only a foot or two away. Fucking here we go . . . I threw myself at the shield, my whole damn body weight. A heavy boy. Big time. I kicked, punched and screamed. The momentum of my offense knocked the three of them right back. Not over, but right back. This gave me extra courage. I thought I could defeat them. This wasn't so bad. I pictured Sick Boy's face on the shield. I punched it so many times, my knuckles bled. They thumped me hard with the shield, knocking me towards the back of the cell. I went to run at it again, but I didn't notice that he'd tilted the shield, so the bottom was pointing towards me like a blade. As I charged, the bottom of the shield smashed my shins. Tactics.

'ARRGGHH, YOU CUNT,' I shouted.

He continued to smash into me until I was pinned to the back wall. I struggled with every ounce I had left, but I wasn't moving. Two leather-gloved hands reached around the shield. One from each side. Before I could work out what they were doing, they secured both my arms. And, as that happened, I felt the shield pressure release. Before I could even look at the screw in front of

129

me who had the shield, he grabbed the back of my head and pulled me forward. As he did that, the other two screws who had grabbed my arms, twisted them up into wrist locks. It started to feel familiar – I was being bent up.

'ARRGGHH, ALL RIGHT,' I screamed, as they twisted up my arms.

It fucking killed. It felt like my arms were being popped out of my shoulder blades and my wrists were going to snap.

'Prisoner, don't move!' I didn't plan to.

The sound of his voice was stifled by the helmet and balaclava he had on. The screw barking at me was the one who had the shield and now had my head. I heard a lot of movement and pushing and shoving. Other people were coming into the cell. It was tight enough as it was. But as they had control of me, I guess it was time for them to take a breather and evaluate the situation. I heard a massive sigh from the screw holding my head.

'Are you OK, Thomas?' he asked. His voice was clearer but still not perfect. There was a lot of noise. The movement I could hear was another screw coming in to remove the helmets from the ones who'd wrapped me up. I suppose they thought the threat was over.

'Yeah, wonderful, except them CUNTS are snapping my fucking wrists! ARRGGHH,' I yelped.

'Ease off, fellas,' he ordered the other two.

Everyone was panting. Fucked. It's a physical game, being inside. It's like you got to be a fucking athlete. Believe.

'Thomas, the officers holding your arms are going to apply cuffs. This is for your safety and the safety of the staff. If you fuck about, we will apply pain to the wrist locks. Do you understand?'

'Yes, Guv.' I'd had enough. My shins were killing me. My wrists. Everything. I just wanted it over.

The straight-arm locks were turned into back-hammers, so my wrists were being held in the small of my back.

'ARGH, fuck!' I yelped. It was an uncomfortable position to be in. The fact that I was still bent over while my head was held down heightened my anxiety even more. I'm not afraid to admit, I was fucking scared.

'They'll be on in just a minute.' Easy for him to say.

I felt the cold metal touch my wrists, followed by the familiar clicking sound of the cuffs locking shut. There was some whispering and things happening that I couldn't see and it was freaking me out. My whole body ached – every part of it. Plus, I was exhausted. Being bent over with the cuffs on was an added stress I was growing tired of. I was being compliant. Why the hell was I still in that position?

'The fuck is going on, Guv? I'm doing fuck all now.' I couldn't hide the wobbles in my voice.

The man on my head didn't answer. He was obviously the gaffer who was supposed to be communicating with me. He just carried on whispering to someone else. My guts were going again. Maybe they were going to give me a good fucking shoeing. Maybe that's what it was all about and they were whispering about how they were going to do it – or, more importantly, how they were going to cover it up. I started to shiver with fear. Each second felt like a fucking day. Not minutes or hours – a day. Maybe they were like Sick Boy. Maybe they wanted to do that to me. Fucking animals. Why would they keep me like that, bent over, cuffed and silent? Talking behind my back. What the fuck? Well that ain't happening. No way. No cunt will ever do that to me again.

I started to struggle. 'You want some, let's have it, you pussy-holes.' I felt ready again. COME ON.

'Whoa, Thomas, hold it there. Don't start fucking around. I'm finding out if I can walk you to the Seg instead of making you shuffle all the way there in this position. I thought you were complying, but if not . . .'

'Sweet, Guv, I'll walk. I'll behave!' At last, I knew what the hell they were doing. I didn't even realise I was going over to the Seg.

It was obvious, really. You kick off on the Unit, you go over to the Seg. But I'd spent most of my time over there, so I wasn't that up on how it worked on normal location. A bit of communication wouldn't have gone amiss. Another minute or so passed.

'OK, Thomas, I'm going to let your head up, so you can stand straight. The two officers holding your wrists in the cuffs are going to support the sides. This is NOT to cause you pain or discomfort. You will be walking in cuffs, and it is to protect you, do you understand?'

'Guv.'

'Good. We are going to walk at a nice slow pace from here to the Segregation Unit. Once there, we will strip search you and bed you down for the night. If you fuck about just once, I will drop you to the floor, place you under full restrain and carry you there. It's as simple as that. Got it?'

'Yes, Guv.' He slowly let my head up.

I couldn't believe my eyes when I saw it was Mr Byrd who was giving me the orders and who had taken me out with the shield. As mad as it sounds, I felt let down. Hurt. I thought he understood me and there he was taking me the fuck out. Of course, he had a job to do, just like everyone else. I hadn't recognised his voice because of the noise, his stifled and firm orders and all the adrenalin pumping around my veins.

'Cain, look, any fucking around and I will take you down. Again. You do understand, don't you?' he asked once more, only this time looking me straight in the eyes.

'Yeah.' I was upset. He could see that. He didn't pick me up on not addressing him properly. Think he let it go because of my shock.

'I'm going to lead the way; you and the two officers supporting you will follow. There are quite a few people outside the cell. Don't worry about all them. They're not here to cause trouble but to make sure you've been handled correctly and everything is being dealt with correctly. We're just going to walk, nice and slow.' He looked at the screws over my shoulder. 'OK, lads, let's move.'

133

They held my arms lightly. A soft touch, just so I knew they were there. We started to walk outside the cell; I heard some more kicking on the doors in recognition. Once on the landing, it felt like a million eyes all rushed on me at once. There was a nurse, a Governor, an SO, a PO, some females doing fuck knows what. But there was also a load of people standing there with clip boards, papers and all sorts of shit. As I glanced at them, they all looked down trying to avoid eye contact. As if I was poison.

Mr Byrd looked around. 'You OK, lad?'

I nodded. Every cell door has a metal flap on it, which can be shut so the inmate can't see out. Most of the time they leave them open, but I could see they'd been shut. They didn't want any boys standing at their doors, trying to watch what was going on. Every fucking flap was shut except one. Vic's. I'd had some bangs of recognition as we walked slowly past the other cells. They could hear us. In my warped mind, that made me feel special. Then I noticed Vic's cell. Fuck. Open for him to see. I was being placid. I'd had my scrap. Done my thing. I just wanted to get to the Seg and sit back. I didn't want to fight any more. But I wanted the boys to think I'd scrapped all the way down there in true Cain style. I was hoping, just praying, that Vic was not at his door.

As I got closer, I saw there were one or two other flaps that hadn't been shut. Perhaps the screws forgot them. Or, more likely, the boys had kicked their doors so hard, the vibration had eventually opened the flap. That happens.

They should have checked before we walked down there, though. Should have checked.

I closed in on Vic's cell – he was standing there in all his glory, staring. Although I could only see one of his eyes and part of his face (because of the shape and size of the spy-hole), we got firm eye contact. I was walking relatively peacefully. Wanting to get out of there. Besides, it's not as if I made it easy for them. I'd fought. Believe. I'd made a rod for my own back. Fighting like that since day one over the Seg; taking out Vic in the manner that I did. I had a reputation to live up to. He stared at me – I could see his delight at my cooperation. I knew he'd be putting it about the Unit in no time. Trying to take my crown. Fuck. I needed to do something about it.

I looked at Byrd walking in front of me. He had his back to me, obviously, but every now and then he'd turn around just to check. The two screws on my arms were barely touching me. Everyone thought it was over. I THOUGHT IT WAS OVER. I looked around, very calmly and slowly. No one even noticed. They'd had their fight. I looked at Byrd in front of me, again. Then back at Vic.

I'm the fucking boss, fool.

'COME ON, THEN!'

I charged forward, easily managing to escape the touch/hold of the other screws. I ran the few paces to Mr Byrd. Even though I was cuffed and, as it goes, I liked him, I didn't care. Image. Wanker. Before he had a chance to turn around fully, I launched a diving head-butt at the side of his face. With my weight and perfect, lucky connection, I knocked him clean off his feet. I nearly fell over myself, I had launched myself with such ferocity, but I managed to stay on my feet. I got a glimpse of Vic. His look had changed to recognition. Fear almost. No, not fear – he was too mental for that. But with an applause to my madness. But the look was one that held other things, too. He knew I was off-key, but that didn't perturb him. He still wanted the crown back. But I'd given a show and I knew it would be all over the jail. Perfect.

The other two screws decked me. I don't know how, all I know is that I was eating the concrete in a heartbeat. Mr Byrd got to his feet. The two screws who jumped me were applying pain to my cuffed wrists. I was struggling like fuck.

'STOP FIGHTING,' one of them ordered.

'Get him up,' Mr Byrd ordered.

I got a look at him. His face was red like a beetroot and was already starting to get lumpy.

Calmly he said, 'You've had your fucking chance now.'

I was lifted up, right off my feet. I was in a seated position, being carried by the three of them. My full body weight rested on my cuffed wrists, which was indescribably painful.

'Right, let's fucking MOVE.' Byrd was tired of fucking around.

They practically ran me off the landing. The stairs were a bit more tricky. They had to be careful not to drop me. But, saying that, I bet they wished they had. We were down in lightning speed. Someone ran ahead to unlock the door and gate which led outside the Unit. It was some woman who was flapping to do it. We were charging at her. If she hadn't done it in time, I swear we'd have mowed her down and smashed right through the door.

The night's cold air hit me as we got off the Unit. We didn't go around the route. Oh no. Straight across Myer's pretty, green grass. I guess that is the correct route when you're carrying some bastard boy.

I heard loads of cheers and shouts from the guys at their windows. They couldn't be covered up. I looked around to see them all, making gestures and screaming. I was famous. In charge. The one who got noticed. I was in agony. I was bruised and battered. I'd even attacked Mr Byrd when I hadn't wanted to. But all that mattered to me was the show. Spoken like a true performer. Only I wasn't a star. And I wasn't in the Albert Hall, either.

DEATH BY EVE, LIFE BY MARY

'What do you want me to say?' I was being flippant.

'Cain, it's not about what I want you to say, I just need to know I can trust you if I relocate you back to Mars-Unit?' Myers never seemed to get agitated. No matter what I said or how I said it.

I'd been given a 'cool-off' period in the Seg. That's what Myers had called it. Another poofy way of describing the dishing out of punishment. Cellular Confinement (CC) but he found those terms 'archaic and of no relevance to the establishment and atmosphere that he was trying to develop'. I was pleased. It could have been a whole lot worse. They were talking about getting the Old Bill involved for the assault on Mr Byrd, only he

138

was sound and didn't want to take it further. Funnily enough, they didn't really talk too much about the damage I'd caused. Just that it was 'inappropriate behaviour' and if I had a problem, I should talk to someone about it, blah, blah, blah. Myers thought that he was getting to the bottom of the problem with his softly, softly approach. When if the truth were known, I was laughing my nuts off at getting away with it.

The punishment may have been fuck all. But I was in tatters from the fight. My whole body ached like fuck and my shins were a rich, red-black from top to bottom. I'd never had such a solid bruise in all my life. They didn't just hurt to touch, but they hurt when I stood up. I felt every ounce of my body weight. It killed me.

I'd done my three days cool-off and it was time for me to go back to the Unit. But Myers wanted this chat first. He liked these chats. The personal touch. But what was I supposed to say to his stupid questions? There was only one answer I could give, 'Course I'm ready to go back, Guv. You didn't need to keep me over here in the first place.'

He sat back in his chair and took a sip from his steaming cup of coffee. He looked at me as if he were weighing up my last sentence. Like he was psychoanalysing me. He definitely fancied himself as a bit of a shrink. I mean, it's not as if my last remark was a deep, Freudian comment.

'Well, Cain, damaging prison property and assaulting an officer is not something that can be overlooked.' No shit, Sherlock.

He fiddled with his thick, grey beard the whole time. I began looking around his office, daydreaming. He took so fucking long to get to the point, I was getting more bored by the second.

'Well?' he asked.

Fuck, he was expecting an answer, 'Yeah, of course I'll behave.'

He looked at me, confused. 'Have you been listening to a word I just said?' No, you daft, old sod.

'Of course.' Liar.

'Then you understand why you have been in the Segregation Unit and why I must be sure you're OK to go back?' Like a broken fucking record.

'Guv, I ain't doing that shit again. Sorry and all that stuff. I'm sweet. Is Mr Byrd OK with me going back over there?' I felt bad about him.

'Well, of course. He's a great officer, you know. He was only doing what he was ordered to do that night. It was nothing personal, you know that?' He was hitting a nerve. The old fool was better than I thought.

I looked down and twiddled with my thumbs.

'Do you?' he asked again.

'Sweet, Guv.'

I'd seen Mr Byrd once since the incident. He spoke to me but he had an air of disappointment to his tone. I guess he was the only one that had actually thought there was something decent inside me. The rest of them just thought I was a shit bag who wasn't worth wasting time on. That I had no morals and would rob a pensioner for a fiver and stab anyone who crossed me without a second thought. Most of them were right. That is who I was. I had no reason to be any different. Nothing to make me want to see life any other way. Since my barricade and assault on Mr Byrd, it was like he'd kind of given up on me, too. Which hurt. Yeah, hurt.

'So, I have your guarantee that there will be no more of this silly business, once you're back over there?' He was serious, too. Asking a child criminal to give him a guarantee?

'You got my word, Guv.'

'Good. Now, before you get back to normal regime, I have two visitors here to see you. You don't have to see them if you don't want to, but I think it would be very much worth your while to do so. Maybe it will give you a different outlook and perspective on things?'

I was clueless as to what that meant. Myers was into restorative justice crap. That's when the victim, or family of the victim, gets to see and speak to the criminal. It's supposed to get the criminal to face up to what they've done. It couldn't be that, though – I hadn't been convicted of anything yet. But I thought a visit would keep me occupied until lunch and, besides, I was curious.

'I'll see them, Guv. Who is it?'

'That's great, Cain. I'll walk you over to visits myself.'

'Who is it?' I asked again.

'Oh, I'll leave that to when you get there. I think that would be best.'

'Ah, a surprise. BLUT, BLUT.' I was excited.

'Erm, not exactly a surprise; more like an incentive to concentrate your mind on succeeding in things.'

I was intrigued. 'Lead the way, Boss.'

Myers went back to his office and left me in visits with a couple of screws. There wasn't anyone else around. It wasn't visits time, but Governor Myers had sorted this little encounter out personally. His jail, his rules.

Maybe it was Emma, I thought to myself. But then, my social worker could come in anytime she wanted. It didn't need to be all cloak and dagger. Maybe it was some sort of special education, or news that my case was being dropped. None of that rang true – none of those things needed to be so covert.

'Lift your arms up,' one of the screws said before patting me down. Normal procedure before a visit.

'Think it might be the Queen who's come to give me a pardon?' I was jumping around like a jester.

'Mmm, someone's come to give you something, but it definitely ain't that.' Deadpan.

It was a short walk from the search area out to the visits hall. Normally there were quite a few screws working there. But as this was a 'special' occasion with only me and my visitors, only two screws were sent to man it. I bounced down the corridor. I had a spring in my step. I'd convinced myself it was good news. Something exciting. It was nice to have a surprise waiting for me.

I got into the hall and saw two people sitting next to each other. It was an old boy and a bird. They had their backs to me. Somehow he looked familiar. They were sitting down but it was clear they were smartly dressed. He was grey and balding; she had rich, brown hair. Looked very glossy. The light from the room kind of sparkled as it hit it. Without seeing her face, I guessed she was younger than him. They looked very business-like. Official.

My jovial bounce quietened when I saw them. I started to get butterflies. It didn't feel like a nice surprise any more. Although there were only the two visitors sitting there, somehow they were giving off a seriously tense aura that filled the room.

They must have heard me come in, as I hadn't been quiet. Never was. But neither of them looked around.

I got to the table and stood right in front of them. 'You come to release me?' I asked, making light of it.

They both looked up. I stared at him first. Fuck, where do I recognise him from? He had a cropped beard – long stubble, but it was shaped. He looked like George Michael. Familiar. He looked at me and said nothing. I turned to her.

'Hello, Cain.' No, it couldn't be.

I looked, then looked again. I rubbed my eyes in disbelief.

'Lily, what the fuck?' I was confused. She looked so different. Beautiful. More beautiful. Less sket. More Cheryl Cole.

'Less of the language, lad, please.' He wasn't aggressive, just mature and adult. Her dad. Shit. I knew I'd seen him.

Never met him, but seen him in the distance when I used to hide up the road, waiting for him to go.

'Nah, I ain't doing this.' I started to walk off.

'Cain, please, we need to talk,' she said.

I stopped dead and looked back at her. I loved her. Shit. I was delighted to see her. But hurt. Painful. Love. Bad. I walked back and slowly sat down. I looked at them in turn, neither of them spoke. There was an awkward silence.

'Well, what do you want?' I leaned back in my chair, putting my hand to my mouth. I was guarded. Concerned.

'Why have you not replied to any of my letters?' she asked. She had an air of calm about her. She seemed different.

'Fuck, Lily, you were the one that blew me out,' I said flippantly.

I'd written to her shitloads when I was in the Seg. Professing my undying love. Thinking of her was what got me through the dark nights of detox. Then I got the 'Dear John' letter from her. She didn't see a future for us. Who could blame her? But I fucking did, for a start. I was broken-hearted. So when she wrote me further letters, I rarely got past the first couple of paragraphs. I was stubborn. Big time. I thought if I read them and got upset, I wouldn't be able to cope. It was a self-preservation thing. Everything is intensified a thousand per cent when you're confined to the four walls of your cell. I couldn't take any more upset, so I didn't read them and I didn't reply to her. In a couple of the letters, I'd seen that she wanted to see me but I refused to send her a VO. I couldn't take it. As much as I really wanted to see her, deep down, I just didn't think I'd be able to cope.

'Don't you swear at my daughter.' He got aggressive, pointing his finger at me.

'Yeah, what you gonna do, blood?' I jumped up off my chair, opening my arms to offer him a challenge. Fight first, think later.

The two screws came running over, 'Thomas, what the hell you doing? Right, visit over.' They went to lead me away.

Her dad, the screws and I were all arguing – firing all sorts of abuse at each other.

'STOP,' Lily screamed.

Her voice and distress made us all stand still and look at her.

'Please, Cain, I just want to talk to you for a minute. That's all I ask.'

I looked at the screws who had hold of me and then at her dad.

'OK,' I said. Then I turned to the screws, 'That sweet, Guv?'

'As long as there's no more jumping around and gobbing off,' one of them said.

They let go of me and I sat down. Her dad did the same.

'Alone, Dad. I need to do this alone.'

'Sweetheart, I'm here for you.'

'Dad, I'm fine. Just go and sit over there with the

officers.' She looked at the screws. 'Is it OK if my dad sits with you?'

'That's fine,' they answered. 'Come on, mate. We'll make you a brew. We're only a few feet away,' they said, reassuring him.

Reluctantly he got up. 'I'll be just over there, darling,' he said to Lily, while bogging me out the whole time. I didn't take my eyes off him. Didn't want to back down and look the coward. Showman. Cock.

'So, why have you been ignoring me?' she said again.

'You serious? You blow me out, then want to rub salt in the wound. I don't need that on the road. In here, it's bad time. Believe. I don't need your shit on top of what I got to deal with in here.'

'Cain, you've been thrown in jail for killing TJ. How the hell is that a basis for a good relationship?' There was an air of sarcasm to her voice.

'You're just gutted you can't be with him any more, innit.' That's all I was bothered about, whether she still wanted to be with him. Even though he was dead, he was still coming between us.

'It's got nothing to do with that, Cain. You're in prison. You killed someone. The reason I can't be with you is because of YOU and no one else.'

We both looked down and contemplated her last remark.

'He was gonna stab me, Lily. Fuck, you told me that the same day. He came at me, I had to defend myself.'

'I heard how it went down. I'm sorry. I'm so sorry about

all of it. I never wanted it to turn out like this. I thought it was all a game . . .' She started to cry. I'd never seen her like that. Never. She was always a tough bird. A bitchy person who did what she wanted when she wanted. Sket looks, bottle-blonde hair. And here she was, brunette, classy and speaking like a lady. Fuck, she'd changed. For the better, yeah. But it was different. She was vulnerable. I'd never seen her cry, never seen this side to her.

'You didn't put the knife in his hand and you never made me go looking for him.' I found myself trying to reassure her. Her dad looked at us and saw she was crying. He didn't come over. I guess he thought this an inevitable part of our meeting.

'Maybe if I'd been a bit more subtle when I told him about us.' She wiped her tears. 'I gave it all the bullshit, Cain, but I really loved you. I wanted to be with you full time. But he threatened to burn down my house while my family slept there. He threatened to kill me and all sorts. I was scared, as much as I made out I wasn't. I was so scared of him.'

'Why didn't you tell me?'

'How could I? You were out of your nut the whole time. You were living on the streets as well. I didn't know what to do. Then he filmed himself . . . with me, you know. I couldn't take it. I hadn't slept with him for months. Refused. Then you and I got closer and closer and then all this happened . . .' She was inconsolable.

'Everything all right over there?' one of the screws yelled.

'Sweet, Guv. Can we have some tissue, please?'

He brought a box over and handed it to Lily. She sorted herself out.

'When's your trial and stuff?' she asked.

'Don't know. I don't even know what the official charge is going to be. My brief is working on it. I ain't got a fucking clue. I'm just trying to survive in here.'

'You still taking?' she asked.

'Nah.'

She gave me a funny, disbelieving look. 'I'm not, Lily, there's fuck all in here anyway. It's not like big-man jail for drugs. Even if I wanted to, I couldn't. But I don't. I feel pretty good being off that shit.' And that was the truth. 'It was fucking hell when I was coming off it, though.'

'You said so in some of your letters.' I blushed. I was so out of it, I didn't really remember much of what I had said.

'It's OK,' she said, 'it was all quite sweet! But I could tell you were pretty out of it.'

'You clean?' I asked.

'God, yes. It was a wake-up call, all of this. I was living a disgraceful life. My mum and dad have been great, though.'

I looked over to her dad with the screws. In all honesty, he seemed all right. He looked wealthy, but grounded. He chatted with the screws freely and he most definitely loved his daughter. He had all the patience in the world. She had put him through some shit. Believe. Me, TJ, the drugs – it's every man's worst nightmare to have their daughter mixed up with all of that. But there he was, at The Well with his daughter, because she needed to see me.

'Look, Lily, I've found all this fucking hard, with you. I was bang into you, you jogged me on and now you're here. I don't want to sound harsh but why are you trying to mess with my head?'

'I just wish you'd responded to my letters and stuff.'

'What is it?'

'My dad contacted Governor Myers personally. They even met before today. Myers thought it would be good for you to see me. Hear what I got to say.' She wasn't really listening to me.

'Why have you come?'

'I still can't believe that you are in front of me here, now. The Governor said it would ultimately be up to you, whether you came or not. He said he couldn't make you see me but that he'd put it to you in a way that he thought might encourage you.'

'Encourage me?' And Myers had done that, the old dog.

'He told my dad that you'd been "challenging", so he was keen to try this to help get you on the straight and narrow. I mean, I know how a "challenging" Cain operates. I bet you've been a nightmare.' I smiled at this last comment. I liked it. Image.

'He didn't tell me it was you. He just told me that he thought seeing this anonymous visitor could be "good for me". I'm still not sure how.'

She went quiet and started playing with her hair. She

was fidgeting. She looked like she had something to say, but didn't know how to say it. She looked over to her dad, who happened to make eye contact with her. He nodded as if to say to go ahead with what she had to say.

'Lily, get on with it. This is starting to do my nut in.'

'I'm pregnant,' she blurted out.

'And? What the fuck that got to do with me?' I was all defensive.

'As much as you think I'm some dirty sket, I'm not. You're the only person I've been with in ages.' She seemed genuine.

'What about TJ, and all the others I heard about?'

'I told you, I didn't sleep with TJ for months and months. And all the others were a load of bullshit.'

'I never heard you deny it.' And that's the truth.

'It was all a front, Cain. A load of crap to make out that I was in control. I felt like the woman. But, the truth be known, you're the only one I've been with in a long, long time.'

I frowned and looked at the table. Fuck. Fifteen, in prison and now this. I curled my lip and felt confused.

'Cain, I'm pregnant and it's definitely yours.' Her words rang in my mind, like the four-minute warning.

CIRCLE OF CRIME
(GHOSTS)

I couldn't hear the dawn chorus of birds yet. It was earlier. A lot earlier. I'd woken in the middle of the night. Again. It was weird. It wasn't the normal turn-over-and-check-the-time kind of waking up. Or the one when you need a piss and a drink. This was different. Mental. One minute I would be in a perfectly deep sleep. Sound. The next, it was as if someone had hit a button in my brain. I'd be wide awake with no chance of falling back to sleep.

I sat up on my bed and I felt out of breath. It was like I'd been running. The more I panted, the less air I could get in my lungs. The less air I could get in my lungs, the more I panted. I thought I was going to suffocate. I jumped out of bed struggling to breathe. Well, thinking I was struggling to breathe. I paced up and down the cell and to my window. I undid it as best I could. I climbed on to the windowsill, put my face in the gap and breathed in with all my might. I couldn't even feel the air going down my throat. Not one bit.

'I can't breathe,' I said to myself.

I knew I could, but when I started to panic, there was no reasoning with myself. I literally felt like I was dying. The whole jail was dead silent, too. A really scary, loud silence. A silence you could hear thumping in your eardrums. All the boys were asleep and most of the night screws were, too. The jail was in the middle of nowhere, so I couldn't even hear any town noises. There was just a close thump that went on in my brain. It rang so loudly, it was deafening. Fuck, I can't breathe.

I started hearing things. The thumping silence turned into shouts and screams. People, enemies calling my name, wanting to kill me. The shadows became mental shapes and, in my weird state, I started seeing faces within them. Shit. Bad. Fuck. I heard Sick Boy laughing. I could see him looking at me. Leering. Sick. Dirty. Horrible. Animal. Die. Die. Die.

I saw myself smoking smack with TJ looking on, laughing. Only he didn't look alive. He was every bit as dead as I had left him. The hallucination was vivid. The final stare he had given me before I ran off was looking down at me. He had the grey film of lifelessness. His skull was cracked. Blood seeped down his head. The glassy-grey look of his dead eyes. The laughing. Stop. STOP. Fuck, I can't breathe.

I paced up and down the cell. I needed it to stop. I was dying. They were killing me. Help me, help me. I pulled at my vest and boxer shorts. I felt their laughing and leering eyes burn deeper into me. Like they were getting inside me. Under my skin. I wanted to burst. I was going to burst. I couldn't take it. Why? Help. Please. I pulled off my vest and started beating my chest, trying to get the pain to stop. It wasn't working.

Shaking like a leaf, I went over to the wardrobe and reached to the top of it. I couldn't find what I was looking for. I got a chair so I could see what I was doing. It had to be there, it had to. I was struggling to support my body weight as I climbed up. I was having hot and cold flushes. I felt weak. I was dying. No air, couldn't breathe. I managed to scramble myself on to the top, but it took everything I had. I looked around the wardrobe, but there was a shadow that prevented me from seeing anything.

'FUCK,' I shouted.

I felt around as quickly as I could. Nothing. I would have known if it had been found. I managed to calm myself down enough to realise that I just had to scan the top slowly. Very slowly. At last, the touch of jagged plastic. The relief I felt was immense. I grabbed it and jumped off the chair and sat on my bed.

I clutched the broken plastic plate like it was my saviour. My God. The sharp edge felt good as I touched it. It was so fucking sharp. Believe. Broken plastic was mean. Perfect. As I looked down, the light hit it and I saw crusty, dried blood covering it. I'd been using it for quite a while. I touched it again, in an almost loving way. And then I hacked at my torso like a madman. I cut myself over and over. As I did so, I tore off some scabs that had barely healed from the last time.

With each attack, I felt a release. Something that felt so blissful and calming. The screams eased off, the faces returned to shadows and the air returned to my lungs. The attack slowed as everything around me returned to normal. One, two more cuts and release. I put the plastic back on the top of the wardrobe. I dabbed the blood with a maroon T-shirt I kept for that very purpose. You could still see the blood, but it was less visible at first glance. I felt better. I put my vest back on, climbed into bed and fell into a peaceful sleep.

The smack of the spy-hole being flipped open woke me up. 'Breakfast, Thomas, start waking up,' Mr Byrd shouted through.

That was my wake-up call, like all the other lads. We had a few minutes to get ourselves up before the screws came back to unlock our doors so we could go down and get some breakfast. I whipped my blanket off and jumped out of bed. I felt really happy. Good. Wired. I went over to the sink for a quick wash. I pulled my vest off, just like anyone else would do.

'ARGH,' I yelled.

The cuts I'd made a few hours earlier had started to

scab and dried blood stuck to my vest. I'd forgotten. Like I always did. It wasn't just a secret from everyone else – it was almost a secret from me, too.

It was my dirty secret. My means to an end. I felt a horrible fear that I couldn't get rid of. It was too much for me. Like every bad thing that had ever happened to me, it decided to attack me deep in the night. And there were shitloads of badness in my life. Believe. Ghosts, man, fucking ghosts. One time I started punching myself. Literally beating myself up. In my rage, I snapped one of my dinner plates and had then cut my chest with it. It was instinct. Not a plan. Second nature. And in that madness, it felt good. It relieved my night terrors.

All the shit I'd done – drugs and booze I'd consumed – mixed with an inner guilt and a longing for some sort of normality, played havoc with my mind. My lonely mind. My night-time thoughts. Self harming was another coping mechanism that I chose – no, was forced to use.

I got a flannel and dabbed the wounds as best I could. There were some hard scabs, some open cuts and some torn-off scabs to deal with. I did the best I could to slow the seeping. As I did it, I felt even more guilt for mutilating my body. I vowed never to do it again. Just as I did every time. It was like a bad one-night stand, or a junkie having one last hit. Another addiction. I didn't do it every night. Sometimes I managed to sleep through. Thank fuck. So my body did get some sort of rest. In the morning, I found it ridiculous that I needed to do something like that. I found it almost unbelievable that I had had to resort to it. But when I was in the panic, there was no other choice.

I put on a clean vest, two T-shirts and a sweater. I didn't want anything seeping through my clothes. Last thing I needed was for it to be found out, on top of everything else. I heard the keys being forced into my cell door.

'Breakfast's up, son,' said Mr Byrd.

Our relationship had returned to what it was before. A little bit better, if anything. We put the other shit behind us. Well, he did. A proper man. Big time.

'Sweet, Guv,' I said, as I walked out of the cell.

'Cain, blood, wait up,' shouted Apples.

Raj, Apples and Vic jogged to catch me up.

'We got to get over the gym for football this afternoon, innit. That cunt Beady and his crew are going to be over there. We need to hit them hard, blood. We got to do this now.' Vic was always up for a scrap.

Beady was a black South London maniac who was in for double murder. Shot two men, point blank in broad daylight. When the police raided his place, he was only a few seconds away from being shot dead himself. Beady was sixteen. Mad, yeah. Sixteen.

He was on Venus-Unit and had a load of his wannabe Yardie crew there as well. He was crazy. And, word was, he wanted my blood. Wanted to fuck me up as soon as he got the chance. Him and his crew were gonna do me and mine. Not just take the Unit, but the whole fucking jail. Be the big man.

'Fuck it, blood, I can't be bothered. He's chatting shit

anyway. Boy's a fool. Just wants to make a point,' I said.

'Nah, blood, he's gonna fucking . . .' Raj piped up.

I interrupted him, 'Nah, cuz, not interested. You boys wanna go looking for it, then crack on. Me, I can't be fucked. It's all hot air.' Maybe I should have let Raj finish. But when I made up my mind, my lot knew not to keep bothering me.

We walked downstairs to the dining hall and sowsh room. Coco Pops. Fucking love them. You were normally only allowed one fun-sized pack. I managed to nick three that day. We sat down to eat. Apples had four apples. You could have as much fruit as you wanted. That's why he was called what he was called. There are worse things to be addicted to!

'Seriously, Cain, you gotta bang that fool out. Cos if you don't you'll look the pussy-hole.' Vic was starting to push it a bit. He could see I was changing. That I didn't want trouble any more.

'I don't give a fuck, it's all bollocks,' I said.

'It's not; he's gonna fucking do you,' he responded quickly.

'We'll see.' I dismissed it as a load of old shit.

I wasn't interested any more. Since seeing Lily, things had changed. Myers was right about that. But it wasn't some romantic fairy tale and I wasn't reformed. Far from it. I'd started hurting myself. I had issues. One minute I thought she was a lying sket, the next I believed her and wanted to marry her. Even though I was only fifteen. And in prison. I'd fantasise about setting up home with her, having the baby and us living happily ever after. I just had to deal with a murder case first. When she told me about being pregnant, she didn't say that things were going to work out between us and that we'd skip off into the sunset. No. But she definitely had feelings for me. I was fifteen, though, and in prison, and she was seventeen and pregnant. Together, all we'd achieved was breaking the law, getting addicted to drugs and getting banged up – each of us in a different way. Not the best start in life.

Her dad agreed to let Lily see me to tell me about the baby because he thought it was the honourable thing to do. He was a decent man. But he wasn't opening his arms to me, so I could be with his daughter. Far from it. He just respected his daughter's wishes and allowed her to be straight with me. He had sorted her right out. She was different. Clean. Normal. A different class. Not the sket I used to know.

So we weren't back together or anything like that. But we did write to each other. Like I said, sometimes I loved her, sometimes I hated her. And that was reflected in our letters. I think she felt the same about me. But there was a connection. Right or wrong. Love can be a funny fucking thing.

And my outlook on life was different now. I did think about being a dad. I did crave normality. I didn't know what was going to happen with Lily, if anything. She promised that I would be able to see our child. As long as I stayed out of trouble and sorted myself out. And that was a motivator. It gave me some sort of direction and a reason to get my head down and go with the flow. It wasn't always easy – I was still interested in maintaining my image. But, for the first time in my life, I was thinking about others.

'What you got this morning?' Apples asked me, as he chomped through his personal orchard.

'Mechanics.' I fucking hated mechanics. They had a workshop where you could learn how to fix cars. I wasn't good with my hands. I loved to draw but since I'd smashed Vic up over there, the teacher refused to have me in her class. I never got in trouble for it and Vic never grassed but, of course, everyone knew. I wasn't exactly quiet about it either. At least mechanics was something, though. And it ticked Lily's box in terms of trying to sort myself out.

I stood by the Unit entrance, waiting to be searched before I went on the morning route to mechanics. The boys filtered out and went to their respective places.

'Morning, luvvy,' Miss Webber was doing the pat downs.

'Morning, Miss.'

I put my arms up so she could do the rub-down search. She did my arms then patted down my chest and stomach.

'OUCH, FUCK,' I jumped back.

My wounds were still fresh. They hurt like mad.

'What's wrong, love?' she said, all concerned.

There was another screw on the gate who looked around, as did a few of the boys in the queue behind me. I'd made quite a fuss. I couldn't help it, it hurt.

'Ah, nothing, Miss. Just been doing a lot of in-cell workouts. Press-ups and crunches. I'm aching, that's all.' Quick thinking.

'I thought I'd hurt you or something!' If only she knew the truth.

She finished her search and I stepped outside. I did love Myers' grass centre. Even though it was in a nick, fuck it looked good. I looked up and saw the sun shining. It was a beautiful day. I was still in the shade from the Unit building. I walked quickly so I could get out into the open.

The route was busy, as it was every morning. I was in my own world, trying to get into the sun. I came to the end of the Unit, stepped out of the shade and tilted my head up with my eyes closed. Beautiful. The warm sun on my face was divine. Believe.

CRACK!

I felt a vicious burning in my jaw. It was so painful it went through my head and all the way down my spine. My legs gave way and I collapsed in a heap on the floor.

'FUCKING PUSSY-HOLE!' Beady was standing over me, victorious.

A split second later there were five pairs of feet stamping down on me. Kicking the absolute fuck out of me. Sometimes in a fight you don't feel the pain until after. That wasn't the case then. I was in agony. They were stamping me to death. Jumping on me and all sorts. Beady started kicking my head and stamping on my face. He totally obliterated my nose. It exploded. My bottom lip was hanging off and my eye was pissing with blood. I felt it all in slow motion. I heard the prison alarm begin to ring and the sound of screws shouting. The last thing I remember was seeing Mr Byrd dropping Beady like a ton of bricks. I was totally fucked on the floor. Mashed up, proper. I still felt the odd stamp and kick as I slipped into unconsciousness . . .

NO MORE EATIN'
4 YOU NOW, BLOOD

I t was my lower back that hurt the most. Funny really, as I think that was the only part of my body that wasn't hit or stamped on. It was the hospital bed. Fucking awful. I'd been there for days. Sleeping on my back the whole time was hell. Along with being continuously cuffed to a screw, it wasn't my idea of a nice break from jail.

I'd lost shit loads of weight, too. Bastard broke my fucking jaw when he belted me. I couldn't chew a thing. And my hunger never stopped! My nose was broken. But the thing that concerned them most was the bleeding. They struggled to stop it. I had got into the danger territory of bleeding to death. All from my nose. Believe.

That shit was bad. You don't need to lose a leg to bleed to death. Plus, I was delirious. Concussed like a mother-fucker. I didn't really know my own name for the first couple of days. They scanned my brain and suspected my old thinker was bleeding at one point, too. That would have meant curtains. Curtains or becoming a cabbage.

I felt so weak. Like death. Sure, my body ached from the beating. Big time. But the weakness and recovery were hindered by my lack of calories. I had no strength in me whatsoever.

When I woke up, the screw cuffed to me was snoring his head off in a chair. I didn't recognise him. When a con is in hospital, you can end up with anyone attached to you. It's overtime for them. You have to have two screws with you 24/7. One of the two is cuffed to you, the other just sits there. Twelve-hour shifts and then change. Fucking boring for them, even worse for me. At least they were getting paid for it.

'You all right, love?' Miss Webber was the second screw.

'Yeah, as good as I can be. When is the doctor coming around? I wanna get back to The Well. Had enough of it in here. The food is shit!'

She laughed, 'I'll go and find out.'

As she got up, she knocked the other screw's chair, waking him, which pissed him off.

'Fucking, silly cow,' he mumbled under his breath. She was well out of earshot. 'You fancy going down for a fag?' he asked me.

'Yes, Guv, love to.'

'Come on, then.'

He was from big-man jail. Needed the overtime. We walked past Miss Webber at the nurses' desk.

'You can't take Cain for a smoke. Governor Myers has a no-smoking policy.' She was dead serious and wasn't going to bend the rules.

'I won't tell if you don't,' was all he replied. We didn't even stop to acknowledge her. He was cool as fuck. A tough bastard that played by his own rules. I could see that he was thick skinned and hardened from the years he'd spent pounding the prison landings.

As we walked off the ward, I got loads of stares. The public are always uneasy about seeing someone in cuffs. Even worse if that someone is a minor. As much as I was a big lad, I still had a baby face. Well, not babyish, but I guess you could tell I was under eighteen. The stares made me feel the big man. They looked at the screw like he was some sort of bullying scum for being cuffed to a weak and innocent child. He was one big geezer, too. Fucking huge. Towered over me. So they gave him dirty looks. He didn't give a fuck. He'd spent a lifetime being looked at like a piece of shit. It was nothing new to him.

We walked outside into the smoking area and he pulled out his Marlboros. Not lights, the real thing. Harsh. Thick. Strong. He passed me one and we began to smoke. I nearly choked on the first lungful. It was the first fag I'd had in months and months. He sucked so hard on his the cherry was about half an inch long within a few seconds.

'What's it like in big-man jail, Guv?'

'Shit.' He was a man of few words.

He had a red complexion and a barrel chest. He was a lump of a man who didn't seem to be bothered by fuck all. And he smoked like it was his last chance to have one, ever.

'I know it's shit, Guv, but do you get a lot of bend ups and stuff?' I was just interested in the fights. Kid.

'Loads. Believe me, son, change your fucking job when you get out of The Well, cos a life inside is a mug's game,' he said it with sincerity.

He threw his butt on the floor and lit another one. I hadn't even had half of mine.

'What did you do?' He'd not bothered to read my file.

'Er . . .' I looked around. 'I had a fight with some boy and he was, er . . .'

'He's dead.' He finished my sentence for me.

'Yeah.' I looked around to see if anyone was listening, even though I knew we were the only people out there.

'Did you go after him to kill him?' He was point blank, no fucking around.

'No, well, not really.'

'Yes or no?'

'Well, I knew he was going to do me, so I was carrying a weapon.'

'You attacked him first?'

'No, he dived on me. He pretty much took me out, then was gonna stab me up. I didn't even see it coming but I reacted.'

165

'You stabbed him first?' He was an old pro. He'd heard stories like mine a thousand times.

'No, I whacked him with a bar and that, well, that . . .'

He interrupted, 'Killed him.' He liked to finish my sentences. 'Any witnesses?' he asked.

'A few. Think most of them have said it went down that way.'

'Manslaughter. Out in five. Tops. That's if you're unlucky.'

'Well, they're trying to pin murder on me. I've been kept in the dark with all of it.' I was intrigued to hear his opinion.

'How old are you?'

'Nearly sixteen.'

'Oh well, even better. Thought you were older than that, with the size of you and all. You won't even do the five, trust me.'

'Didn't you realise I'm a YO? It's on my paperwork,' I said.

'Listen, son; this overtime – to me, this is a job. I couldn't give a monkey's toss who I'm bed-watching, so long as I get my overtime.' Couldn't get more honest than that.

All the talk of sentences and crime made me focus on the time I'd done already and what was left to come. When might I get to see Lily and maybe have some sort of life? I started to think of TJ. And that final, life-ending crack when I hit him. I started to visualise his face. It sent shivers down my spine. I felt bad. GUILTY.

'Cain, what you doing smoking?' It was Emma. She smiled gleefully.

'Emma!' I was really pleased to see her. I'd not seen her in ages.

'You've been in the wars a little of late. How are you feeling?' she asked.

The screw just carried on smoking and switched off to our conversation.

'My body is battered, but turns out to be nothing serious. Although the prick bust my jaw, so I've not been able to eat. I'm fucking starving.'

She looked at my nose. It was still huge and swollen, and both my eyes were black. 'That looks sore,' she said.

'It's difficult to breathe but, other than that, it ain't too bad. But it's giving me the needle being in here. It's so fucking boring. When can I go back to The Well?'

'I spoke to Governor Myers and all of the boys that assaulted you have been shipped out to different jails.'

'So he does do disciplinary moves, BLUT, BLUT.'

'Of course he does, Cain, but only as a very last resort. And judging by your injuries, they bloody well deserved it.' She looked a little upset by my disfigurement.

I looked down to see a paper bag in her hands. A McDonald's bag. 'SHIT, that for me, Emma?' I was so excited.

'Well, you can't eat. Your jaw.'

'Fuck that, I've dreamed about this!'

She looked to the screw. 'Is it OK if he has it?'

'Fill your boots, love, I couldn't give a shit.' No people skills at all.

She gave me the bag and I began to salivate like mad. A Quarter Pounder with cheese, two double cheeseburgers and fries. Lots of them. And a Coke. Heaven. I just sniffed at it, taking in the beautiful aroma. I can't tell you how nice it smelt. How much I wanted that food. My favourite in the world. I undid the first double cheeseburger. It was like a work of art in my hands. I went to take a bite.

'ARRGGHH,' I yelped, as I opened my mouth too far. My jaw was in bits.

'You OK? Maybe you shouldn't have it.' She went to take it from me.

'NO,' I shouted. 'I'll be fine.'

She stepped back and let me continue. I broke the burger up into small pieces and pushed them in my mouth. Oh, the taste. It was so fucking good. I could barely chew it, so I just moved it around my mouth, breaking it up as best I could. It was going to take a long time to get through it but I enjoyed every second.

I sat on my bed, so stuffed I felt ready to pop. The screw I was cuffed to was struggling to keep his eyes open again.

'So, he'll be able to go back tomorrow?' Emma asked Miss Webber.

'That's the impression the nurse gave me. She said the doctor will be around shortly to confirm it, but things are looking good. As long as he carries on taking the antibiotics for the infected cuts on his torso.'

I guess cutting your body with a dirty piece of old plastic isn't the best thing you can do to yourself.

Emma looked at me with worried eyes. 'I think you need to talk to someone about that, you know.'

I was really embarrassed. 'I'm fine. They were just, er, a couple of washing scratches.' It was the best I could come up with.

'Cain, it's something we need to talk about when you're ready. I want to see you well – not hurting yourself.'

Miss Webber and Emma went quiet – respectful in a motherly, sisterly way. The male screw wasn't listening to fuck all.

'Right, I've also got some news about your case. I spoke to your brief earlier and the CPS,' Emma said.

'At least they talk to you,' I answered.

'Well, there's some good news. Well, not good, but things are looking a lot better. It looks as though you will be charged with manslaughter, not murder, now they've done all their investigations. They're just waiting on one or two things and then it will be made official.'

I should have been happy, but how can you be happy when you're going to be charged with manslaughter? Yeah, I killed the boy and I didn't deny it. But it wasn't murder. It wasn't nice and I shouldn't have done it. But I didn't murder the boy. I didn't.

'I know it's not great, Cain, but reducing the charge will have a dramatic effect on your sentence. It will be minute in comparison. And I think it's fair, for once. It is what you have already admitted to.' She was right.

I saw the male screw look up and smile with his thumbs up, nodding. Seemed like the old sweat knew what he was talking about after all. But I just couldn't get excited about being someone who's been convicted of manslaughter. I was thinking more and more about that actual night. I was starting to understand the implications of my actions. I'd taken someone's life. It was dawning on me, however slowly.

FIRE WALK WITH ME

I stood in the queue, waiting for the phone. There were three boys in front of me but I wasn't that bothered. We had plenty of sowsh time left. I clutched the photo of Lola tight in my hand. She was twelve weeks old in the picture. She had beautiful blonde hair that fell in ringlets and she already had a cheeky smile, just like her mother's.

I gazed at the photo, like any other loving dad would. But, there I was, sixteen and in prison for manslaughter. My trial was all over very quickly. I pleaded guilty and all the witness statements pretty much added up to what I said. One or two details were different. But then, I was out of my skull at the time. The judge had said, 'It was a vicious and heinous act that you committed. And you must bear some of the responsibility for being in that situation. The life you were leading wasn't honourable or decent and I will make sure that is reflected in your sentence. A young man is now dead, Mr Thomas, and his death was inflicted by you, no matter what the charge or what the surrounding factors may be. You will have to live with that burden; you will have to live knowing that his blood is firmly on your hands.'

I hadn't been sentenced straight away. There were various reports and shit that needed to be done by the jail, my YOT worker and Emma. I was made well aware that my conduct inside was going to have a massive impact on what my sentence would be.

Since getting back to The Well after the hospital, I'd gone with the flow. I'd had one or two scraps in the toilets, that sort of thing. Part and parcel. Always happens in young man's nick. I had to make sure that boys didn't fuck with me. I didn't want to be seen as some pussy-hole weed. Especially after the fucking hiding I'd taken on the route. There were a few attempts from boys trying to take me out. Not from my own crew. I could see Vic's dick growing but he was biding his time. I could see that. I just focussed on doing my bird and keeping my nut down so I could get a fair sentence and be on my way out of that shit-hole.

I hadn't seen Lola in the flesh yet. Lily didn't want to bring her to the jail. I understood. Lily never came back to see me either. But we wrote to each other and spoke on the phone a couple of times a week. We were getting close. She was having a huge impact on my behaviour. For once in my life I started to feel like I had a real purpose. I'd created someone. Made a kid. I had a real blood tie that I was dead proud about.

The last couple of times I'd called Lily, she wasn't able to talk to me, though. If it wasn't Lola she was attending to, it was her college work. Yeah, the girl was studying. Her parents gave her loads of support. Good. At least my daughter was in a good place. A rich place. The best of everything and well looked after. I knew Lily was a busy girl, so I didn't let it bother me. I longed for the day when I would be out, though, so I could see, touch and kiss my beautiful daughter. And Lily, if she gave me the chance. One step at a time, son.

I was at the front of the queue at last. Both the phones were being used. I was starting to twitch with excitement. A few minutes more and I would be talking to Lily. Come on, come on. I looked at the clock then back at the phones. YES – one of the boys was off the phone. I walked towards it but some kid jumped on it before me.

'Nah, blood, it's my turn,' I said politely.

'Whatever, fool, I'm here, innit.' New boy; didn't know me.

I grabbed him by the throat, 'Watch your fucking mouth, blood, and get in the fucking queue. YEAH?'

One of the screws came running over and pulled me off. 'Get the fuck over there.' He pushed me away and I went flying. It was Manning, a screw who'd transferred from big-man jail. He didn't fuck around. He could handle himself, but didn't bother with the bullshit rules.

'What's going on?' he said to both of us.

'Fool just went for me.' The kid clutched his neck as he said it. Give him a round of applause, ladies and gentlemen.

'Guv, I've been queuing for the phones for ages. He jumped in front of me, trying to mug me off. I want to talk to my family.' First time I'd called them that and it felt good.

'True?' he asked the other fella.

He stuttered as he tried to think of something to say in his defence, 'Er, well, I was, he was, actually . . .'

'Shut up, you stumble bum and get to the back of the queue.' He turned to me, 'And you keep your fucking hands to yourself. Anyone does the grabbing around here, it's me, understand?'

'Yes, Guv,' I said.

Just like that. Resolved. The wrong screw and there would have been bend ups, nickings and all sorts.

I picked up the phone and dialled Lily's number. I knew it so well – it was the only number I ever rang. I was shaking with excitement. I'd dialled it so quick, it felt like ages before it actually rang. At last. It was ringing. It rang some more. And more. Shit, they weren't in. Again. Just as I was about to hang up someone answered.

'Hello?' It was her dad.

'Er, hello, Mr Davies. Can I speak to Lily, please?' I was always as polite as could be.

'Huh . . .' he sighed deeply, then went quiet for an uncomfortable amount of time.

'Mr Davies?'

'She's not in, Cain.' I could hear the frustration in his voice.

'Oh. Will she be back in the next half hour, because I've not got that long left of association. I've not spoken to her for a while.' Hold it down, son, hold it down.

'No.' Nice answer. Rude cunt.

'OK, when will she be around to speak to me?'

'She won't.'

Deep breath. DEEP BREATH.

'Mr Davies, I know you don't like me . . .'

He interrupted, 'You got that right.'

I paused, then started again, 'I know you don't like me but I do have a child with your daughter and, unfortunately, I will be a part of her life for some time.'

'Over my dead body.'

'What is that supposed to mean?' I raised my voice slightly.

'I'm not having you anywhere near my daughter or granddaughter. You're scum and I hope they throw away the key.'

'I'm her FUCKING DAD,' I raised my voice.

'You're nothing but a sperm donor, so don't start thinking you're anything more than that.' He was cold as ice.

'Yeah, let's see what Lily has got to say about it. PUT HER ON,' I demanded.

'She doesn't want to speak to you.'

'I said, PUT HER ON.' I was losing my cool.

'What you going to do, Cain, kill me, too? You're a fucking joke and, as long as I'm alive, you won't come anywhere near my family.' He meant what he said.

'Then WHY THE FUCK did you come here and WHY THE FUCK has everything been OK until now?' I was desperate.

'I had to let my daughter get her foolish thoughts out of her head. She felt she was doing the right thing by telling you and keeping open a line of communication. But she's come to her senses now.'

'LET ME TALK TO HER, YOU PRICK,' I yelled.

He cleared his throat, 'You are a fucking degenerate with nothing and nobody. You are scum. DO NOT CALL HERE AGAIN.' He hung up.

'Hello? HELLO? HELLO?'

I started smashing the fuck out of the phone, 'YOU FUCKING, DIRTY, FILTHY CUNT . . .' I screamed as I did it.

'Whoa, the fuck you doing?' Manning grabbed hold of me.

'Man, get your fucking hands off me!' I shoved him off.

He let me calm for a second, 'You can have that. But you raise your hands to me again or damage property in front of me, I'll bounce you all the way to the Seg.'

I was seething. I clenched my fist. The red mist was closing in. I looked at Manning deep in the eyes. He was serious. Calm, but serious. I thought better of it.

'Now fuck off and enjoy the rest of sowsh, yeah?' he said.

I nodded at him and walked off. I went back into the sowsh room. A load of boys were playing table tennis and video games.

'Shit, what was that all about?' asked Apples.

'Her fucking dad won't let me talk to her.'

'Nah, blood, that's heavy.'

The fool I had a row with at the phones came up to me, 'Come on then, big man, think you're it, I'll smash you up.' He offered me out.

'Fuck off, blood, you don't know who you're fucking with.' Apples talked for me.

'Shut up, you little cunt, or I'll smash you up, too.'

I palm-punched him in the chest, knocking him over a chair. 'Suck ya mum!' I shouted.

I felt my collar being yanked back. 'You've had your fucking chance; you're going behind your door.' Manning had been watching me.

'Get your hands off me, you prick!'

He gave me a sharp push, 'Move yourself. LAST CHANCE.' He was ready to bend me up.

Vic came out of nowhere and had an evil smile on his face. He seemed to enjoy my fall from grace. I walked out of sowsh and headed back to my cell. I kicked walls and threw my weight around all the way back. Manning followed me, not paying attention to my hot air and violent outbursts.

He unlocked my cell door. 'I don't know how you

normally behave but, I'll tell you something, you fuck me around like this again, it will be the last thing you ever do.' He wasn't used to kid bullshit.

'Yeah, FUCK YOU.' I grabbed the door and smacked it into him, cracking the side of his head.

He grabbed the back of my head and dropped me straight to the deck. I'd never been taken down with such force. My nose started bleeding like fuck. Since my kicking, all you had to do was look at my nose the wrong way and it would bleed.

'The FUCK do you think you're doing?' he demanded. 'COME ON!'

'Two choices, you calm the fuck down and I let you go, or I drag you to the Seg.' Calm. He'd done this a thousand times. He took no shit.

I stopped struggling, so he slowly let me up. He saw the blood on my nose, so he went into my cell and got some tissue.

'There, pinch it with this.' He helped me stop the flow of blood.

'You need to see anyone?' he asked, meaning a doctor.

'No, Guv.'

'Right, I'm going to shut your door and forget this happened. I think that's the best all round.' He had every right to nick me and take me to the Seg, but he gave me another chance.

'Sweet, Guv,' I said, deflated.

He left my cell and shut the door. I pulled out my photo of Lola. I looked at my walls covered with photos of

Lily and Lola together. Like a cassette, I played out my conversation with her dad, over and over and over. 'You're scum.' I imagined Lily and Lola together and that bastard laughing at me. Cunt. Animal. FUCK. My daughter. My family. MY FAMILY. Deluded. I started to kick the fuck out of my cell. I smashed it all up. The table, the chairs, the fucking lot. I was in such a ferocious temper, I didn't stop until everything was in a thousand pieces. I fell to my knees and starting sobbing. I cried and cried and cried. The one and only piece of hope I had was gone. I'd lost my purpose – my reason to be a better person. So what was the fucking point in trying?

THE BAD FACTORY

I knew he didn't have the ball but I barged into him anyway. Prick was going to get dealt with. Since the altercation in the sowsh room, he'd backed off – he had heard what I was about. And since then my attitude had nosedived. I was slipping back into fight mode. I'd lost my focus and reason. The system was wrong. Fuck the world. I was right. I'd toyed with the idea of happy families and all I ended up with was a broken fucking heart. Again.

There had been a rise in sickness among the staff – assaults had gone through the roof and it wasn't just me. Boys were getting tougher. Banging screws out left, right and centre. So they went off sick. The more they went

180

sick, the less we got out of our cells. The less we got out of our cells, the more we'd attack the screws when we did. Out of frustration.

Riding your time behind the door ain't pretty. Believe. It wrecks your mind and fucks with your emotions. The only saving grace inside is the time you get out your cell. Take that away and you've got a bunch of bad kids boiling away in cages. That happens, there's going to be fucking riots. What's the answer? Fuck knows. That ain't my job. Just telling you how it was.

I was riding bang up shit loads and it was killing me. I'd started cutting myself again, too. Mr Byrd had put me on self-harm watch and tried to talk to me about it. Not in some muggy way, like I was a kid. He listened and didn't patronise. Turns out the man knows a shedload about depression. He didn't take the shrink route, just the worldly approach. Kind of related it back to personal experiences and shit. I listened and it helped. He recommended exercise. The only time I'd ever done any of that was when I was running from the feds or chasing some fool to smash them up. He took me to the gym, though, and I started running and lifting a few weights. And then I got into football. Became addicted to it.

With fitness and when things were going well with my baby-mum, I was happy. Then the shit and the fan had to speak to each other again. Fuck. My anger and roughness had returned. It was my way of dealing. I tried to block out my family. I ripped up all the pictures. Decided to fight. I still used fitness to ease the night-terrors and panics. It worked. It was my medicine. But then the staff shortage meant gym shortage.

I used to beg to be taken over there, just for half an hour at a time, but I wasn't allowed. Gym was a privilege. But it was my fucking medicine. I needed it. So, the more they said no, the angrier I became. The angrier I became, the more the evil panics returned. And then, BAM, I started to self-harm again. I wasn't doing it as much as before – I was trying to control it. But the longer I went between episodes, the more ferocious my self-attacks became.

I was a boiling pot of anger. But, in a small way, I still had the good voice in my head trying to level me out. It was saying, 'Hey, come on, this ain't the way to go.' Some have their evil twin sitting on their shoulder, encouraging them to do bad. It was the opposite for me.

But that fool from sowsh had bugged me. After a couple of days, I'd got over it, though. Vic hounded me about it.

'When you gonna bust him up, cuz? Why ain't you done it yet? You pussy-hole, or what?' is all he'd say. Bang up followed by more of the same was my excuse. But I knew he could see I wasn't the same bad man as before. I was trying to be a nasty piece of work, but it wasn't true. On the outside, I was being as vicious and causing as much mayhem as before, but now I had a conscience. Yeah, a conscience. That was the fundamental difference. I knew what I was doing was wrong. Before, I didn't think about fuck all. I didn't care about anything. But I'd come to learn a bit more about right and wrong and what was important. So inside, I was different. I had an inner battle to try and be the big man. It wasn't coming naturally.

What I'm trying to say is, I was forcing myself to be bad. I knew I was doing wrong and, even though not many people would say I was on the road to recovery at that point, it was actually a giant step forward in my rehabilitation. Most would have said I'd taken a fucking long jump backwards. Regression of the tallest order. But I was starting to feel, and that was a really new experience. And it all started when I found out about being a father. FUCK.

Although I had that inner turmoil, I chose to do what I thought I did best – hurt people. I was trying to be good at it again and, on that football pitch, I was kicking that fool from sowsh all over the place. It was the first time we'd had gym in a couple of weeks. It was magic. Fucking magic.

Vic, Raj and Apples were with me – Vic was egging me on the most. 'Fucking do the cunt! Why you tapping him?' he said to me after my big tackle.

'The screws will see,' Apples jumped to my defence.

'Who's asking you, you little black cunt?' Vic was starting to be nasty to Apples. A lot of the time.

Apples had told me that that was how it used to ride, before I'd taken Vic out. Things seemed to be slipping back slowly. Vic was getting a lot braver with me, too. He could see I'd lost my natural violence. He was the one person I most wanted not to notice. But he had. So I had to work double hard to show him otherwise. He never said anything. Actions speak louder than words, though, and he was slowly moving back into top spot. I had to stop it.

'Don't fucking speak to him like that,' I said, in my most menacing voice.

'Or what?' The first challenge from Vic.

'Whoa, boys, we're on the same team here,' Raj jumped in.

Vic had been found guilty and he had a new air of I-don't-give-a-fuck. He was banged up at fifteen for being the leader of a drug ring. Fifteen. Plus they were still building a case against him for running a prostitution ring – pimping out girls as young as fourteen. And adults. And he'd been fifteen. This boy did have a lot in common with TJ. Only Vic was a million times worse. He didn't give a fuck. He was looking at a lot of years when he got his sentence.

I saw my boy on the ball again, so I ran into him, did a dirty tackle and elbowed him straight in the snot-locker.

'ARRGGHH,' he yelped, as he crashed to the floor. His nose was pissing with blood.

I booted him. 'You fucking pussy-hole!' I said.

'I'm sorry, please, I'm sorry about before.' He looked up at me and I felt terrible. Yeah, terrible.

The gym screw blew his whistle, 'Right, that's it. Game over. Cain, step away.'

I looked down at the guy on the floor in front of me and gave him a shrug that said, 'It's over, don't worry.' I looked around and saw my three boys, so I toughened up once more. 'YOU FUCK WITH ME AGAIN,' I said loudly and, looking at them as I did so, 'I'LL KILL YOU.' The showman. I needed Vic to think I was the same. What a fucking bullying wanker. All the boys headed inside to get changed and go back to the Unit for dinner.

I'd had a shower and was drying myself off, as were the other boys. We weren't rushing. We had an afternoon of bang up to look forward to. The gym session was a one-off. It was back to short staff and bang up. The thought of it was destroying me. Running around made me feel alive. But playing the big boy was doing me in. I wished I could speak to Lily . . .

'I'm fucking sick of this shit, man. Bang up is doing my nut,' Raj spoke the words that we all thought.

I started to get dressed.

'Let's do something about it.' Vic had an evil grin on his face.

'Yeah, let's smash our cells up, that'll show them!' Apples started bouncing around.

I couldn't be arsed with any of it.

'Nah, we got to do something more than that,' Vic said.

'What?' asked Raj.

'Take the fucking Unit.'

'You're mad, bruv,' said Apples.

'The fuck do you know, you little mug.'

'Ease off him, for once, yeah?' I piped up.

'So you up for it?' he asked the million-dollar question.

'How the fuck are we gonna do it?' I asked.

'Dinner, tonight. Refuse to bang up.' Plain and simple.

'They'll get kitted up, blood,' I said.

'What, you fucking scared, or what? The fuck has happened to you? You like being banged up all the fucking time, do you? Cuts on your body suggest you don't.' Below the belt, cunt.

I bit my lip, 'I tell you what I ain't scared of, is you. You speak to me like that again, blood, you'll fucking wish you hadn't.' I bogged him out. He looked away. I still had it when I needed it – I was serious.

'Vic's got a point, blood, let's fucking do it – it'll show them they can't fuck with us any more.' Raj was bang up for it.

They all looked at me. I was fucking angry about being banged up all the time. I thought about Lola. I thought about Lily. And then her dad. I was good-for-nothing scum. I tensed up with anger. Fuck them.

'Fuck it, let's do it,' I said.

It was Friday as well, chips night . . .

THE LONG GOOD FRIDAY

I couldn't believe that bastard had pushed Apples off the roof. Fuck. He'd be dead or crippled to the max. It was no little fall. I knew Vic was plotting to take me out but I thought I had it all nailed down. Fuck, I'd decided to get among this riot to show him and I thought I'd done a crazy good job of it. I'd gone nuts with the screws. But then he was an opportunist. He was one of the only people who could see my weakness. He saw an opportunity when he smashed into me after he'd pushed Apples.

'Time for me to take back what's mine, you fucking pussy-hole. You've had your chance at playing the big man. You're fuck all, and now I'm gonna smash you up, fool.' Vic was ready to fuck me up. I was on my knees, clutching my guts. He'd hit me so fucking hard, it felt like all my organs had exploded.

He walked towards me slowly. I tried to get to my feet again, but my abdominal pain was excruciating, I just couldn't get up. He raised his weapon as he got closer. I really did see evil in his eyes. I was transcended back to when I was with TJ and he was going to do me. It felt the same. Believe. I was shitting it. Only this time, I had no weapon to defend myself; and I didn't have the blanket of drink or drugs to distort my fear. I didn't even have the ability to stand.

I looked around at the other boys. Raj, where the fuck had he gone? The others were huddled together, looking scared out of their wits. Vic had nothing to lose. He was looking at severe time. He didn't give a fuck. Killing me would be the icing on the cake. BANG! Vic's head was hit hard. It looked like a concrete club had totally annihilated him. He went crashing to the floor like a sack of shit. I had been clutching my stomach and wincing, waiting for him to land his fatal blow. But CRACK, he was down. Raj had taken a run-up before landing the biggest punch I'd ever seen.

'You fucking prick!' Raj screamed as he whacked him, 'How the fuck, man? What about Apples?'

Raj started kicking the living fuck out of him. The attack was getting heavier with every kick. Vic had dropped the weapon and was delirious after the first punch. He squirmed around, unable to defend himself.

'Think you're a fucking BAD MAN? FUCK YOU,' Raj shouted.

He stamped down hard on his chest. 'ARRGGHH,' Vic screamed.

'FUCKING PUSSY-HOLE.' He wasn't easing up.

'Raj, he's not worth it,' I barked.

He didn't listen, his blinkers were down. He had one thing on his mind: take Vic the fuck out. And it wasn't about being the Unit's big man. I guess he'd got sick of Vic's bullshit and when I took control that had stopped. And now that it was starting again, Raj couldn't take it. Besides, he loved Apples. We all did. How the fuck could Vic have killed him? Cunt. Animal.

But he wasn't worth it. I could see that. None of this was worth it. It was bullshit. As much as I was trying to be bad, my temperament for it had gone. And now Apples. Fuck! More people were getting hurt. It was killing me.

'RAJ, LEAVE IT, BLOOD. FUCK,' I screamed.

He stopped and looked at me. 'He's a fucking animal, cuz. Piece of shit has bullied us forever. Then it stopped cos the cunt couldn't handle you. And now you don't want it any more, he's taking it back. Look at Apples, man. I ain't letting this cunt do it again.' So more people had noticed I'd gone soft than I thought.

Vic had blood pissing out of his face. I hadn't thought Raj had it in him. Yeah, the boy was in for stabbing someone to death. I ain't saying that he wasn't bad. Shit. It's fucking evil. But when boys are cheering you on and you have an image to protect, sometimes you'll go to any lengths to do it. But I didn't think Raj had the minerals to stand up to Vic. I was wrong. Now I was worried he was going to do something he'd live to regret.

'Fuck him, Raj. He's a dog. A dirty fucking dog that's not worth shit. Enough is enough. You've taken the fool out and that, man, I owe you. Believe. It's over, though. SHIT, LOOK OUT!'

BANG! Vic cracked Raj on the back of his lower leg, dropping him to the floor.

'I SAY WHEN IT'S FUCKING OVER.' Vic was dribbling with blood and rage.

'YOU CUNT, FUCK, ARRGGHH . . .' Raj was in agony.

Vic had used all his energy to attack him. Raj had done a handy job in smashing him up in the first place. I should have been watching. I should have been watching.

I started to crawl over to them. They were only a couple of feet away. Vic was trying to get to his knees so he could smash Raj again. Raj was rolling around and screaming, holding his bust leg. Nah, it can't play out this way. No chance. Every move I made, I felt a ripping and burning pain shoot straight through my stomach. I felt like I was minutes away from knocking on hell's door.

Vic got to his knees. Shit, he was doing it. Raj, not Raj. Nah, blood. Fuck that. I moved as fast as I could. Raj had barely noticed what was about to happen.

Vic raised his weapon, ready to strike and yelled, 'FUCK YOU.' He swung it with all his might.

'ARRGGHH – FUCK YOU, YOU ANIMAL,' I screamed

in agony, as somewhere I'd found the strength and ability to get to my feet and dive at Vic.

I punched him square in his already bloodied face. As I did, I took some of the blow he'd swung at Raj. I punched him so fucking hard, it knocked him the fuck out. I landed next to him. I felt like my insides were hanging out on the wrong side of my body. The pain was incredible. The weapon fell out of his hand, so I threw it as far away as possible. Vic, Raj and I lay there in agony, none of us able to stand.

'ADVANCE!' I heard a shout.

In my semi-conscious state, I saw the roof door burst open and fuckloads of stormtroopers come running through. They were kitted up, shields held high. I saw the other boys getting bent up. Chips on a Friday. Bad, man. I clutched my stomach and closed my eyes. I couldn't fight. I just prayed that they'd have a bit of mercy when they got to me . . .

FAITH

I was in such a deep sleep, I reckon a bomb could have gone off and I wouldn't have woken. But it's a different kind of sleep when you're knocked unconscious from meds or drugs. You pass out but you don't rest.

I had been rushed to hospital when the Tornados stormed the roof. The state of me said it all. I was totally out of it. I was coughing up blood and I was in so much fucking pain. Believe. Even though I'd been one of the perpetrators, they didn't get rough with me. How bad I was couldn't be hid. And, contrary to popular belief, most of the screws are decent people. Most of them.

I don't remember much of the journey over, I was drifting in and out of consciousness. The paramedics and screws in the ambulance were trying to talk to me and that was getting on my tits. For some reason they wanted to keep me awake. I wasn't concussed, but I think they thought I might have had some sort of head trauma. 'Does this hurt, does that hurt?' Yes, love, IT ALL FUCKING HURTS.

My guts were bad. I didn't have any split organs but I did have horrendous internal bleeding. He hit so hard, man. They put me out as soon as I got there. Funny that, they did everything they could to keep me awake on my way there but the minute I arrive, they put me under. I had a your-abs-are-seriously-fucked injury. There was a lot of stitching and pulling about when they operated.

I woke up with a fucking sore stomach. Whatever people say about recovery being worse, I beg to differ. I was in pain when I woke, but nothing like the pain of when Vic hit me. I honestly thought my liver had exploded. The fact that I couldn't get to my feet was unbelievable. I really thought it was all over. When Vic was about to do me with the head shot, I thought that was just a courtesy blow. I thought I was dead anyway. I came fucking close. Internal bleeding isn't a joke, man.

'Cain? CAIN?' I heard my name being called.

I opened my eyes, letting in the pain of morning.

'Come on, mate,' said Mr Byrd. 'You're heading back to The Well.'

'Sweet, Guv. I'm allowed to stay there now?' I asked.

'It's up to Mr Myers but I'm pretty sure you'll be shipped out just as soon as there's a space.'

Bog standard. A riot is more than enough to constitute a disciplinary move. Even in Mr Myers's eyes. Raj and Vic had already been moved. They'd gone to opposite ends of the country. Fuck knows where. But they'd gone. Hospital had prevented me from going anywhere so far.

I didn't want to be shipped out. It was all my fucking fault. Kid. Thick. Chances. I had felt like I had a purpose being a dad. And Lily. Shit. But instead of standing up and being counted like an adult, I decided to become the victim and hit out. I'm not blaming my age, but maybe that was a factor. Fuck knows. We all make mistakes but my young life had been riddled with them. And the minute I was faced with a challenge again, I failed in the worst possible way.

I started to get dressed but it was tricky since I was cuffed to Mr Byrd. I just about managed.

'Do you fancy going for a smoke before we leave?' Mr Byrd was good like that.

'Love to, Guv.' I still smoked when I could.

As much as The Well had become a no-smoking joint, some of the screws still sneaked them in for themselves. And when my behaviour had been getting better, Mr Byrd and one or two of the other screws would let me have a smoke every now and then. They are human.

'Hurry up, then. There's someone who wants to see you before we go back.'

* * *

B&H, a proper fag. I sucked on it hard as I lit it. I know smoking is bad for you and all that but, fuck, it tasted good. Mr Byrd smoked, too. Neither of us said much – just smoked in silence. We were at the point in our relationship where we didn't need idle chit-chat to fill the air. We knew one another well. The other screw who was supposed to be looking after me was sitting on the bench half asleep.

'CAIN THOMAS,' I heard shouted, in an official tone. I shat myself.

I looked around and saw Apples – he was cuffed to one screw and had another with him, just like me. He was giggling his tits off at my response.

'HA HA, blood, you were shook!' he said, mocking me.

'Was I fuck? I knew it was you!'

'Then why did you shit yourself!?'

We embraced each other with a huge man-hug. Loved that fool.

'Easy, blood, watch the arm,' he said.

I noticed his un-cuffed arm was in a plaster cast.

'That your only injury, you fucking poof!?'

'Ha ha, I heard you cried like a baby when Vic pushed me off, BLUT, BLUT.' He pretended to cry.

'Whatever, I was gutted when I heard they had an inflatable to catch you.'

What we didn't see over the edge that day was that the screws had a balloon-type thing to catch roof-top prisoners who might fall. So when Vic shoved him off, it saved his life. They're not perfect, though, and Apples still shattered his wrist when he landed. He needed it pinned and a plate put in, which meant surgery, but he'd survived.

Mr Byrd had told me that Apples was OK when I woke up from my own surgery. That made me happy and, yeah, I think I might have shed a tear or two. I thought he was dead. Didn't realise the screws had all that Hollywood shit. Byrd didn't tell me that Apples was in the same hospital as me. I guess that would have been a breach of security or something. But here we were. His recovery time had been pretty damn lengthy, too. But knowing Apples, he'd have milked it for as long as he could.

Apples turned a bit more serious. 'I heard that Vic fucked you up proper when he hit you.'

I got on my high horse, 'Nah, blood, fucking prick . . .' I stopped, realising it didn't matter any more. The bullshit. The façade. 'Yeah, bruv, geezer caused internal bleeding. Could have killed me, or so they say.'

Apples acknowledged my more honest approach.

'That's harsh, man. You OK now?' he asked.

'Not feeling too hot, but getting there.' I looked at Mr Byrd. 'Just depends where these lot ship me out to.'

'I'm going to Feltham.'

'Harsh,' I said. But then any move would have warranted the same response.

'I've told my parents, which ain't so bad. It's closer for them to visit, innit. You told your . . .' Then he remembered I didn't have anyone to tell. The only family

I had was Lola, who I'd never seen, and Lily who wouldn't talk to me.

I moved on. 'Yeah, they're taking me back to The Well, then I'm getting shipped out. No beds just yet, apparently.'

'Fucking loads of beds at Feltham.' Apples looked confused.

'Can't have you two in the same nick, can we,' Mr Byrd piped up.

'True,' Apples agreed, 'but that ain't the reason you're going back to The Well. They could ship you anywhere. Nah, blood, they got other plans for you.' That set alarm bells ringing.

Mr Byrd looked a little agitated. 'Right, lads, finish up and say your goodbyes.' Mr Byrd was good to have let us have a chance to say goodbye. He didn't have to. Shit, he would have got into trouble if the Governor found out.

Apples knew his shit. It seemed like Byrd didn't want him telling me what my next step was; he wanted this short-lived goodbye to be exactly that.

'Look after yourself, Apples, you're a good lad. Stay out of trouble, yeah. How long you got left?' I asked.

'Only two months, but we'll see if they pin some shit on me for our little protest,' he said it with a cheeky smile at the screws around us. They couldn't help but smile back; he had a way about him. 'Cain, man, fuck all this shit. You ain't this type, bruv. I can see you could have a life. Go get your daughter and woman, man, cos this – all of it – it's bollocks.' The truest words ever spoken and I knew he was right.

'I'll write to you,' I said.

'No you won't,' he snapped back, 'and I don't want you to bother with that. I'm in and out of nick, bruv. It's in my blood.' He pointed at his head, 'Use this, yeah?' Little man called Apples. Cheeky fucker, naughty as hell. Loved to nick things. But, fuck me, the boy knew what he was talking about. He knew the way of the world.

'Right, Cain, let's go.' Last call, Mr Byrd.

Apples and I had another man-hug.

'Be lucky,' Apples said.

'Safe.' I just hoped that someday I could get to see him in another place. Another world. Who knows?

I sat there and bounced my leg up and down, it had become a real habit. A problem, really. It was a nervous thing. A comfort thing. I guess it's better than filling myself full of smack and booze, though.

'Cain, knock it off. Fucking hell,' said Mr Byrd.

'Sorry, Guv.' I started chewing my nails.

Emma gave Mr Byrd a dirty look, she hated bad language. 'Er, sorry Miss, just kidding with him.' Mr Byrd was a bit nervous around Emma. Geezer fancied her; I could see it all over.

I looked at him and gave him a smile in a piss-taking way. It was a bit of light relief, watching him act all gay. We were sitting in Myers' office, waiting for the old hippy to make an appearance. I'd been there for what seemed like hours.

I had been taken straight to his office on my return to The Well. Emma was already there waiting. Governor Myers was always late. In all honesty, that was because he was always doing something for someone. Or attending to something that he thought he could help with. He really was one of those people who believed in goodwill among all men. He saw good in everyone and believed it could be found in even the worst of people. You could say he was in the right job; there weren't many people in the prison service who had his kind of faith. Believe.

'What's going to happen to me, Emma?'

'Like I said a minute ago, Cain, I'm not sure. One thing I do know is, you better be honest and think about what it is you want. Because, knowing Governor Myers, he'll be leaving a lot of this decision down to you.' Ain't that right. Governor Myers operated that way. He'd always try to present you with an opportunity; if it wasn't grasped with both hands, then the only person to blame would be yourself.

'Hello, folks, sorry I'm late. I had . . . Well, never mind, you don't want to hear about all that. Cain, how you feeling, young man?' Genuine. A bit pompous, but genuine.

'Still a bit achy, Guv, but on the mend. Look, Guv, I'm really sorry about all the shit and damage we caused.' I was embarrassed. I didn't want it to sound insincere. Because, for once, it wasn't.

'Anyone want a coffee?' he asked. He hadn't even listened. 'I can't function without a coffee!'

No one wanted one. He had an old-school coffee machine in his office that was always on and always had steaming coffee in it.

'That's how I feel about cigarettes!' I tried to make a joke.

Emma and Mr Byrd gave me a filthy look. I was only joking out of nerves. But it went straight over the Governor's head. He sat down and slurped at his coffee. He leant back in his seat and did his usual stare and psychoanalyse bit. Now this really did go on and on. Put yourself in a place where there's an uncomfortable silence. Double it – shit, triple it and you still ain't getting close to how long he fluffed his beard, slurped his coffee and stared.

'Cain,' finally he spoke, 'I cannot and will not tolerate violence in my prison. You know that, we've been here before, yes?'

'Yes, Guv.'

'Which makes it even more upsetting for me to see that you have been involved in this latest episode of violence and damage. I am not in favour of disciplinary moves but, in this case . . .'

I interrupted, 'Look, Guv, please – I fucked up on an epic scale. But I was really starting to get somewhere. I had my daughter, I wasn't causing any trouble, I was getting my head down. And then . . . God, why do I always do this to myself?' I was getting emotional.

'If you let me finish,' the Governor said, 'but, in this case, I'd be more than justified if I sent you to the other end of the country. There are a few people who think differently, though, me included.'

What the fuck?

'I'm not going?' I said. I tried not to get too excited.

'It's not as simple as that, Cain. There are some conditions. Mr Byrd here has fought your corner and Miss?'

'Just call me Emma, Governor.'

'Emma believes that, until recently, you had been making some decent progress.'

She added, 'Cain has had a life full of dramas. One followed by the next. Yes, he's not handled them all in the best way he could but since he found out about his daughter, Lola, there has been a marked improvement in his behaviour. Until this relapse. Other than that, The Well, and in particular Mr Byrd here, have played an exceptional role in his rehabilitation.' Byrd actually blushed.

Now he said his piece, 'Cain has been a lot better. He has become a great trainee at YOI Romwell and, in all honesty, he's been growing into a decent young man – despite his difficult start in life. He seemed to find his focal point in his daughter and, after an introduction into the gym and personal fitness, together we seem to have found an answer to his reliance on self-harm.' I looked down. I was ashamed.

'You've got a couple of good people here, Cain, which,

believe me, isn't normal in our failing system. Instead of throwing it back in their faces, you should have been embracing it. Which is what I thought you would do, so what happened?' Myers had this way of making you feel bad. He wasn't aggressive; you just felt really bad when you disappointed him. Like you'd upset a granddad or something.

I took a deep breath, 'Guv, please excuse my language here, and you Emma.' They both nodded for me to continue. 'For the best part of my life, I've not given a fuck. I've not cared who I hurt or, when I think about it, who hurt me. I don't expect you to feel sorry for me or anything but I've never had a family or any of that shit, man. None of it, yeah? One place to the next I went, always without question, never being asked. I'm a fucking person. I should have a fucking choice. But I've never had one. And then, when I was with the Sick family, shit . . . Look, I've only ever been able to get through the day if I was in control and, nine times out of ten, that was either by using my fists or taking drugs and drinking. TJ dying at my hands shook me. Yeah, feeling a boy die from my blow was something that made me scared. But then the drugs wore off and, like everything else in my life, I put it to the back of my mind and carried on. Fuck the world. Fuck everyone except me, the big man. And then, Guv, you arranged for me to see Lily.'

'I thought the meeting was a great way of making you see that there is more to life. I took a gamble, Cain; it could have gone the other way. But I believed it would work, I believed in you.' He looked at me right in the eyes.

'It did work, Guv. More than I'd have thought. Seeing Lily – finding out about her being pregnant, and then Lola being born. I'm not saying that it made me perfect. I'm not saying I stopped being bad. But I started to realise that everything has a consequence. Every action I take has repercussions, good and bad. Shit,' I started to cry, 'I started to feel, man.' Emma put her arm around me. 'I know I ain't perfect; I know I'm fucking scum. What man would want his daughter near a piece of shit like me? But hearing that direct from Lily's dad hurt me. Shit, killed me. Just when things were going right, when I was starting to stand up and be counted, I was knocked and I took it like a fucking coward.' I was crying, bad.

'What's this?' he asked Mr Byrd.

'Cain was having contact with Lily and then all of a sudden it stopped. He made a call, her dad told him that Lily never wanted to speak to him again and then he never heard another word. From that point on . . .'

I jumped in, 'I decided to be a cunt again, Guv. I thought that maybe her dad was right. I am a fucking animal who has no point. No reason for being on this earth. So I decided to be bad again. Live up to my reputation.'

'And that's what I can't . . .' the Governor tried to answer me, but I hadn't finished.

'I know you can't have it, Guv. But none of your rules can make any difference or make me change. It's me. ME that can change things. And when I decided to go bad again, it wasn't the same. As much as I wanted to be the big man and be in charge, I couldn't. Because I feel. Now I FEEL. I can't be the person I was any longer.'

I couldn't talk any more. I put my arm around Emma as I sobbed. Myers and Byrd were quiet for a few minutes until I had got hold of myself.

'Thank you for your honesty, Cain. It takes real bravery and I commend you for that. Maybe if more people took a leaf out of your book and lived by their word, things could be better for everyone. I'll put my cards on the table.' This was it; I was going to find out where the hell I was heading to. And I mean that in every sense of the word. 'Mr Byrd has done everything in his power to support you and to keep you here at The Well. He sees good in you, which proves that you most certainly are not scum. I want to keep you here and, as much as I'm not one for moving trainees, I would experience the wrath of my superiors if I didn't move ALL trainees who were part of a huge, concerted indiscipline. Unless I had an exceptionally good reason. I'm spearheading the restorative justice programme for young offenders. I've been liaising with the court, Youth Offending and Emma here. They all agree that, in your case, you'd be perfect for the programme. Plus, it would have favourable implications on your sentencing when it comes up. But don't think that your recent violence will go unpunished – it won't. You can expect a harsh hand coming your way on that. But before I decide whether to put you in this programme, I wanted to see if you really are in the right state of mind for it and, more importantly, whether you actually want to change for the better.'

'I do, Guv.'

'I believe you. And with all the supporting information from Mr Byrd, I want to offer you the chance to stay here and do this programme. If you want to?'

'Of course I want to, Guv. You can count on me.' I paused, 'What is restorative justice?' Say yes first, ask what it is second. I still wasn't quite an adult.

SOUL 2 SOUL

I was totally saturated in sweat. Every part of my skin leaked; it wasn't just my armpits. My clothes were so wet it looked as though I'd been swimming in them. I'd been running on the treadmill for fifty-five minutes. I was hanging out of my arse. Fucked. Just had five more minutes to go.

This was my medication. I felt alive when I was exercising.

I'd not self-harmed for ages. I had been given a job as a gym orderly. I loved it, man. I used to spend most of the day over there. I'd have to clean the place, equipment and everything. I used to make it spotless. Took real pride in it. It felt like it was my very own gym. I started giving some of the younger boys some basic gym inductions and things like that. It felt like a real job. And because I was over there most of the day, I could workout as much as I wanted. I used to hammer myself. But it made me feel really good.

Reluctantly, I had to take some meds, too. They said I had ADHD. Fuck knows if that was right. I was on Ritalin – shit made me feel terrible. One minute I would feel drowsy, the next I swear that stuff actually made me hyper. I hated it. But I wanted to show willing, so that eventually they'd let me get off it. My dosage was slowly coming down. Besides, when I exercised fucking hard, it was like I was burning off the effects. Don't know if a doctor would say that was possible, but the harder I trained, the more normal I felt. I was in a pretty decent place, mentally. Sick Boy would haunt me at times, but somehow I felt a little bit more in control. More able to lock it away, which helped.

I wrote to Lily a couple of times a week. I sent her VOs but I never got a reply. NEVER. Somehow, I learnt to deal with it. I tossed the coin and put myself in her position. I'd be lying if I said I didn't sometimes flip out about it, though. I'm human. But humans can get angry without killing someone. I didn't bother calling. I knew it was a waste of time. I'd never get to talk to her and it would only have alienated me further; proved that cunt and what he had said about me was right. I was still sickened by him. I tried to put myself in his shoes, her being his daughter and all, but that bastard didn't need to be that way with me. I got no problem with him airing his issues in an aggressive way. But he enjoyed the way he made me feel. He got a fucking kick out of getting to me.

But, I was seventeen years old. I'd kept my head down and got on with my bird. I hadn't become soft on the landing; I just made it clear that I was not in the mix with the big-man mentality any more. I still made it clear that I wasn't an easy target or someone to be messed with, even if I wasn't in the mix for causing havoc. I leave you alone; you leave me alone.

'Cain, they're going to be here in a few minutes, I need you to finish up.' Mr Byrd had come into the gym to collect me.

Shit. I'd been waiting a long time for this – restorative justice. It had taken months to plan. And today was the day it was all going to happen. I turned the treadmill up to sprint speed.

Through panting breath I said, 'Two minutes, Guv, just finishing.' I ran like my life depended on it. Focus. This is it, son.

I towel-dried myself as quickly as I could. As I got dressed, I was still sweating. An hour-long run would always do that to me. No matter how long I showered, or at what temperature, I'd sweat after my wash. But I still felt cleansed. Today I had the added nerves of meeting TJ's parents. Actually meeting the parents of the boy I had killed. Fuck. Serious. Scared.

When Myers told me about restorative justice, I didn't

really consider all the implications. The idea is that the criminal faces up to his crimes. And now I had to go and sit in a room with the parents of the boy I'd killed and talk to them. Find out what they were feeling. I'd heard all sorts of horror stories about situations where the room had erupted into violence; where the con had ended up killing themselves afterwards because they couldn't take the guilt. I knew most of them were probably bullshit. Probably. So I tried not to let it affect me. I put it to the back of my mind and figured I'd deal with it when I had to. As I sweated through my clean clothes, tying my laces, I could no longer put it to the back of my mind.

'Cain, move your arse, for fuck's sake!' Mr Byrd hated being late.

'Coming, Guv.'

I'd put it off for as long as I could. I stepped out of the changing room. There were some boys working out and a couple of gym screws inside. Mr Byrd and I made our way out. I got the token 'good luck's from a couple of the boys and screws.

Mr Byrd unlocked the gate and we stepped outside to walk the route over to visits. I remember the sun shining brightly. It was blisteringly hot. I was already struggling to control my perspiration and it just got worse. The more I thought about it, the more I sweated. The more I sweated, the more conscious I was, which made me think about it even more. I started pulling at my shirt, attempting to fan myself cooler.

Mr Byrd stopped. 'Look, mate, this will be fine. I'm not saying it's going to be easy for you or for them. But it will be fine. You've turned into a good lad, Cain, so don't be all tough in there. And don't be overly apologetic either. Just be yourself and ride it out.' He could see I was nervous.

'What if the old man attacks me, huh?' I was genuinely worried about that. I was a father. OK, I'd not seen Lola but I was still a father. I knew it was a possibility.

'You listen to me – nothing, I repeat, NOTHING like that will happen. Mr Manning and I will be in there and so will a psychologist. If it looks like things aren't going how they should, the meeting will be terminated. Just ride it out. You are not going to be in danger.'

We started walking again. The sun was blinding. I lapsed into deep thought, 'Get me through this. Please get me through this.' I said it in my mind, over and over. I didn't want the walk over there to finish. I was scared. The slight breeze there was cooled my wet skin. I started to get goose bumps. Fear. Adrenalin.

We went into the search area for the visits hall. My heart was racing at a million miles an hour. It felt like it was going to jump out of my chest. I was panting like fuck. My mouth had gone totally dry. I needed a piss. No, a shit. No I didn't. Then I did. Fear and adrenalin were doing the conga in my colon. I felt the colour drain out of me.

'Wait there,' Mr Byrd said. He disappeared for a few seconds, returning with a cup. 'Sip this.'

'What is it, Guv?' I was bouncing with nerves.

'It's just water. Calm down, Cain. It'll be all right. Just sip that for a second.'

I took it from him and downed it in one. Manning came through the door.

'They're both here and waiting,' Manning announced to us.

'What about the shrink?'

'Yep, there as well.'

Fuck, it was really happening.

'Right, Cain,' Mr Byrd said, looking all serious, 'we're going to go in there now. Mr and Mrs June will be sitting at a table. You will go and sit down opposite. Mr Manning and I will be sitting near you—'

I interrupted, 'What the fuck do you mean "near"? Thought you were both going to be there. You fucking told me . . .'

'Whoa, whoa, whoa,' he put his hands up, trying to calm me, 'we are going to be just two feet away; in the middle of the table on either side. So you will be safe. Nothing is going to happen, I can assure you of that. Miss What's-her-name-shrink will be in there, too. Most likely making notes and giving you the odd cursory glance through her geek glasses.' We all had a little snigger; Mr Byrd was good at calming a situation, he could always give me a bit of confidence. 'Just listen to what they have to say,' he continued, 'and go with the flow. Like I said before, there is no one else in the visits hall; it has all been specially arranged by Governor

Myers.' Myers did love to arrange special visits for me.

I took a deep breath and contemplated what he said.

'Ready, son?' asked Manning. He was a big lump, told it how it was, but he had a decent, human side to him. He gave me a caring and sympathetic look. I couldn't speak, so I just nodded.

'It'll be all right,' Mr Byrd's last words before I followed him into the visits hall.

Although I was six feet tall, what I could see when I entered the room was blocked by Manning and Byrd's huge backs in front of me. I slouched a little, trying to hide some more. We walked between empty tables. I faced the floor. I couldn't bear even to look at my awaiting visitors. Every hair on my body stood to attention. I felt a lump in my throat. My guts were doing cartwheels and I shivered from the sweat that still soaked my body.

'Mr and Mrs June,' said Byrd, 'this is Cain Thomas.'

Manning and Byrd parted like the Red Sea in front of me. I felt the visitors staring. I was still facing the floor. I couldn't bring myself to look up. My right leg started to shake at the knee. I just stood there. It felt like forever. I heard the seats being moved as Manning and Byrd sat down. I couldn't bring myself to sit down. Shit, I couldn't bring myself to look at TJ's parents.

'Cain, sit down, lad,' Mr Byrd said.

I took a deep breath and slowly started to lift my head. I looked from my feet to the chair in front of me. From the chair to the empty table and then . . . Shit. My eyes met Mr and Mrs June for the first time. I'd not seen them in any of my court appearances. I don't know if they were there or not. Maybe they were in the gallery. I don't know. I didn't want to know. Maybe, in my fucked up head, I had seen them before but forgotten about it. All I know is that, that was the first time I remembered seeing them through sober and stable eyes.

They were older than I thought they would be. If they weren't pensioners, they didn't have many birthdays to go before they were. He was well dressed, like a golfer. He had thin, silvery/blue hair swept to the side and Frank-Butcher-style glasses. Tanned; obviously took regular holidays. She was motherly. No, grandmotherly. She had trendy glasses and a bob haircut that wouldn't have looked out of place on a woman half her age. But her well-fed frame and old-fashioned clothes made her look, well, grandmotherly. They held each other tightly by the hand. She had a solemn look; his was more aggressive.

'Hello,' I was nervous and it kind of fell out of my mouth. Neither of them replied.

I put my hands on the back of the chair but was shaking like a leaf. I was trying to pull it back so I could sit down but I was making a right pig's ear out of it. Fear can do the wildest things. Manning jumped up and came and assisted me. I sat down, placing my hands on the table. I stared at my hands, then my lap and back at my hands. It was deadly silent until I heard the noise of writing. I looked up and saw the shrink making notes and looking around as she did so. I had no idea what she was writing; nothing had been said. Maybe that was the problem.

'There's not a day goes by that I don't see the image of Tristan's dead face – battered, bruised, unrecognisable. Do you know that?' Mr June started the proceedings.

'Er, Mr June, I, I . . . Er . . . I only hit him once. I didn't batter him.' Fucking TWAT. That's the first thing that came into my mind.

He stared at me in astonishment for a second. 'You fuck . . .' he stopped and composed himself for a second. 'One blow, yes, but the disfigurement to his face that followed was because of that one hit.'

I didn't know what to do or say.

'Imagine having to see your son lying dead on a table like a slab of meat. You can't, though, can you? You're just a kid.' His missus started to sniffle.

'I, I do have a daughter.'

'You have a daughter and you're in here? What the hell is the matter with you?'

It went silent once more. The shrink was making notes. I looked at Mr Byrd for some support. He gave me a friendly nod.

'My Tristan had mentioned you before, I'm sure. I thought you were friends?' Mrs June said.

'We were, Mrs June. I'd known him for a few years – ever since I got to the estate.'

'You went to that bastard school, didn't you,' Mr June said. He looked at his wife. 'I told you to keep him away from those evil sods.'

TJ went to the normal comp but he hung about with us. He always had an unnerving desire to be the worst. He didn't need to. And now I could see the type of parents he had, he really had wasted his life. He didn't need to go down the road he had done. He had family, support and a life that I and thousands of others craved.

'I just want to know how he knew our son, Stephen. Please allow me to ask the questions I want to.' He put his hands up suggesting he'd shut up. She carried on, 'What did you do together?'

I shrugged my shoulders. How could I tell her what we really got up to?

'Please tell me, Cain. I have lost my youngest son; I agreed to do this to get some sort of closure. Please tell me.'

'We used to ride around on our bikes, chatting to people, playing some footy, that type of thing.'

'And taking drugs and bullying people. I know what you lot got up to,' Mr June interrupted.

'Look, Mr June, you're right. We were bad kids. ALL of us. We all did some shit – sorry – some bad, bad things that I ain't proud of. Yeah, we did terrorise people. And a lot of drugs were taken and sold. I ain't gonna lie any more. Radman – Simon – he had the right idea. Joined the army and got the hell out of there.'

I took a deep breath and let my words fill the air. I felt like a weight was starting to lift.

'You took drugs together?' Mrs June asked.

'It's no shock, woman, we knew . . .'

She interrupted, 'Stephen, SHUT UP.' She looked back at me. 'I just want to hear what the boy has to say.'

'Yes, Mrs June, we all took drugs. Lots of them and

drink.' I wasn't going to beat around the bush any more.

'What sort of drugs?' She knew, but I think she just wanted to hear it from me.

'Weed and beer was what we started on, but then it got heavier, ya know.'

'What?' She wanted it spelt out.

'Cocaine, heroin. It was everything; we did everything.'

'But you were so young.' She looked at Mr June. 'Your brother influenced Tristan, I swear.' So that was the secret uncle TJ used to go on about.

'So, if you were friends, what happened?' Mr June seemed to have taken an interest in his wife's questions now.

'OK, this is going to be difficult for you to hear, but I guess that's why you came.' I held my hands tightly together. 'Things got out of control. I mean, WAY out of control. I'd become a full-blown drug addict and alcoholic . . .'

'AT FIFTEEN?' She seemed shocked at that, but she must have known . . .

'Yes, Mrs June, at fifteen. Please, let me tell you this. You do both want to hear it, yeah?' They nodded, so I continued, 'I was a total junkie. I was living on the streets. I can't remember if Clear-View kicked me out or if I left – I was out of my head the whole time. But I was living rough. TJ – there's no easy way to say this – he was drug dealing. Big time.' They tensed up at that remark, but said nothing. I think they already knew. 'I'd been, well, seeing Lily and . . .'

'Lily was Tristan's girlfriend, wasn't she?' Mrs June looked uncomfortable.

As much as I was speaking candidly about the whole thing, I still had to talk with some sensitivity. I couldn't very well turn round and say he was knocking her about and forcing her to have sex. Well, I could have, but I wasn't comfortable with doing that.

'Mrs June, Lily was scared of TJ, sorry, Tristan. She wanted to leave him but with all the drugs he was selling and taking . . .' she winced at that, 'he was unpredictable. We were all scared of him. He'd turned violent, man. Lily and I, well, we started to spend time with each other.'

'You mean you started to knock his missus off.' Mr June was defending his son's honour. And who wouldn't?

'It weren't that simple, yeah. I wish I could say it was. Lily and I, shit, we loved each other.'

'She played the pair of you,' he snapped back.

I fidgeted in my seat. 'Yeah, maybe so, to a degree. A lot of it was a front; she made out she was all that, when really she was a scared girl.'

'Humph,' he gestured sarcastically. It wound me up.

'Look, TJ was nasty. NASTY, you get me? People were scared of him; I was FUCKING scared of him.' I was getting agitated. Mr Byrd gave me a look that told me to calm it. 'I'm not trying to upset you, just, well, you know – tell the truth, for once in my life, tell the truth.'

'All this was over a girl?' Mrs June asked.

Looking back, it pretty much was. It wasn't that simple,

though. There were running tensions between TJ and me for a while. I was bad. He was BAD, BAD. The next level. And I was scared of him. But shit, Lily was the reason for some of that, who am I kidding? Day one we were into each other. I'm no knight in shining armour and I won't speak ill of the dead because they can't answer, but I won't speak fairytale either just to protect their memory. Did he treat like her like an animal? Yes. Could she have left him? Yes. Was I wrong to carry on with her behind his back even though he was bad to her? Yes. There ain't no rights where this is concerned. Only truth and it isn't pretty.

'It wasn't just that, we were both fucked up, sorry, messed up on drugs at that time, too. I guess neither of us was thinking straight. I was told that Tristan was going to stab me up cos he'd found out about Lily and me carrying on, so I was scared.'

'Why didn't you just lay low?' asked Mr June.

'It don't work like that, sir. It's not how things work on the street with our types.'

'What do you mean, "our types"? Tristan wasn't like you.' He wanted to hear the truth but couldn't seem to handle it.

'He was worse, Mr June. I feared for my life because I knew he WOULD kill me if he got the chance.' That resonated with him.

'Why didn't you come to us, or the police?'

'Let's be honest, Mr June, what would you have done if some junkie teenager turned up on the doorstep of your nice house and said, "Excuse me, Mr June, but I think your son is going to stab me up, can you help me please?" What would you have said?' I put the ball back in his court. He couldn't answer.

'What about the police?' Mrs June asked.

'Like I said, it doesn't roll that way . . .'

She leaned forward and took a sterner tone, 'DON'T you keep saying that rubbish. My son is dead. DEAD. So I want firm answers from you.'

'Because I was a junkie. A scumbag. A bastard. A hoodie. Or whatever else you want to call me. I was out of my fucking head on drink and drugs. I was scared and I had a . . . It doesn't matter.'

'No, tell me,' she said.

'I had to protect my rep.' I didn't know where to look. 'I know it's stupid. Pathetic. But that's just how it was.'

It went quiet for a minute or two while everyone composed themselves. BANG! Mr June thumped the table.

'Tristan is dead; you killed my boy. Why, God, why have you done this to us?' He took his glasses off and rubbed his wet eyes. Mrs June put her arm around him. His aggression turned to sadness. I didn't know where to look. I felt my guts churning up. I looked at them. I could see their anguish. Real pain. Cause and effect. I'd killed their son. Even if I hadn't meant to, I'd still done it. A life wasted. A life lost. Taken away. They will never get to see their son again. I'm responsible for that. I'd wrecked the lives of so many. The drink, the drugs, the beatings, the happy slapping, the kickings, the robbing, the sex, the swearing, cursing, hating, maiming, hurting, smashing, destroying, damaging . . . ARRGGHH! My eyes began to fill up.

'I didn't mean to kill TJ, I swear. I never meant to do that to him. Please believe me. I . . . I . . . I was stupid. Fucking MAD. CRAZY. Please, I never meant to hurt him. I thought . . . I thought . . . I thought he was going to kill me.' I stood up, 'He came for me, see?' I did the punching action to the side of my head, 'Took me out when I wasn't looking.'

Manning came over. 'Sit down, lad.'

I pushed him away, in a non-aggressive way. I was crying. 'He pulled out a knife; I was knocked on the ground. I thought . . . he was . . . I knew he was going to stab me up, yeah? Please, I never meant to kill him. I didn't, I swear. I ain't lying.' Manning tried to get me to sit down, but again I pushed him away. I was balling my eyes out, Mr and Mrs June were both really crying now. 'I grabbed that weapon, yeah I did.' I started thumping my chest, 'Cos I was stupid. FUCKING STUPID. I wandered around waiting for the inevitable. I knew he was coming for me. I swear, in my fucked-up brain, the weapon was for my protection. I didn't want to kill him, never even thought I could. Stupid. FUCKING MAD. It didn't cross my mind. Never thought things like that really happened. Please believe, yeah? I never meant to kill your boy. Every FUCKING day I have to live with it. WHY didn't I go to the feds? FUCK. Every day I see his face. I see it. It's there when I wake up, it's there when I go to the gym, it's there when I go to sleep, and it's there in my dreams. There's not a day that goes by that I don't regret doing what I did. NOT ONE SINGLE DAY. If I could change it, I would. If I could be DEAD instead of TJ, I would be. I'm sorry I killed your son.' I wiped my tears, 'I'm more sorry than you'll ever know.'

I sank to the floor and sobbed my heart out. I'd never been more honest and open. EVER. Heartbreak. The only way to describe it. A life of torture and misery. So many lives wasted. Why had I been born? Why was I here? What was my purpose? I had nothing or no one. FUCK. Death. Pain. Hurt. Seventeen years old. Why? Shit. I was on my knees clutching at my cheeks and eyes. I just couldn't stop the tears. Every single bit of pain and suffering I'd ever felt or dished out rushed through my veins. All at once. Every memory, sad and good, every face, friend and foe, flashed through my thoughts in those few minutes.

I felt hands touch my shoulders and the back of my head. I felt the warmth of someone trying to embrace me. Take away my pain. Give me some healing. Give me some love. Fuck. I was blubbering so much. The arms pulled me tight. I looked up to see Mrs June had taken me in her arms. She was crying. Mr June stood over us, crying and unsure of what to do. I was stunned. She pulled me tighter, bodily begging me to embrace her back. I flung my arms around her, pushed my face deep into her shoulder and cried and cried and cried. We held each other so tight, I don't think either of us ever wanted to let go . . .

My eyes were red and sore. I felt like every drop of fluid in my body had been cried away. I was totally exhausted. I barely had the energy to walk. Manning was taking me over to get my evening dose of Ritalin. Normally that got on my tits, but after the meeting I'd just had, it wasn't really registering. He wasn't barking on at me and he only really spoke when I did.

'You did well in there, mate, you really did. I know it can't have been easy. Shit, I don't think I'd have coped with all that. I really admire your honesty, Cain. You can walk away with your head held high.' I really appreciated his words.

'It doesn't change things, Guv, but at least now there is a bit of truth in it all. At least I'm finally realising things matter. I actually do give a fuck.' Shit, I think I was turning into a man, at long last.

He undid the door to the meds room and we walked in.

'Ahhh, did you have a kiss and cuddle with the dead boy's parents?' Bishop goaded me, the fucking animal. He was in there with two boys getting their meds. He obviously felt brave enough to bait me with Manning there. Cunt wouldn't have dared if he'd been on his own. Coward. I ignored him. 'What was it like?'

I looked at him. 'What was what like?'

'Looking into the eyes of the parents of the boy you murdered?'

I killed him. Didn't murder him. YOU FUCKING PRICK.

I said nothing. Manning led me towards the meds hatch. Bishop was standing right beside me. I'd not seen him in a long time. He obviously hadn't got over the time when I made him look like a complete cunt. Actually, I only showed him up for what he really was – a bullying wanker. He larged up to me as I got closer to him. I looked through him. But I felt my blood boiling. Hold it down, son, hold it down.

'Why they wanted to come and see a piece of shit like you, I'll never know.' I was inching closer. He started to move to get in my way – he was looking for a fight. 'Look at you; you don't even have the decency to take it like a man. Blubbering your eyes out in front of them poor people. You're a fucking joke.' He could see the redness in my eyes. He stood in front of the hatch, blocking my way. All of this had happened in seconds. Manning was behind me, just locking the door, although he must have heard every word. The whole room had; the other boys as well.

'Excuse me, I need to get my meds.' I was gritting my teeth, trying to control myself.

'And to top it off, you're a fucking fraggle as well. You're scum, Thomas, fucking scum.' I wanted to rip his throat out.

'I want to get my meds.' I pushed past him. Not too hard, but enough. Exactly what he wanted.

'Fucking push me, yeah!' He grabbed hold of the back

of my head, trying to drop me to the ground.

'THE FUCK YOU DOING?' I yelled, 'I just want my meds, YOU FUCKING PRICK.'

I punched him in the chest, knocking him back. Cunt was trying to put his hands on me and I'd done fuck all wrong.

'GET THE FUCK OFF ME,' I shouted.

We wrestled each other until Manning came over. He shoved me and I went flying into the wall. He grabbed hold of Bishop.

'The fuck you doing, you mug?' I heard him shout to Bishop. 'Get over here.' Manning dragged him to the corner of the room. I didn't hear everything, but it was something along the lines of Bishop having 'more mouth than a cow's got cunt'. Lovely expression. He pretty much had Bishop pinned up against the wall. Manning finished with, 'You got a problem with this, I'll see you at the gate.' Bishop was left looking a complete fool. Again. Nice.

Manning walked back to me. 'Do you really want your meds, son?' I shook my head. 'Then let's get you back to the Unit.'

We walked out and Bishop looked like shit. I had a little snigger. He had been the last person I wanted to see. I looked at Manning as we left the Unit; he really did play the game fair but, fuck, he didn't do things like most of the others. He did it his way. I don't know if it was because he'd worked in big-man nick, or what. I didn't see him after that shift. Heard he had some issues with the job and left. One thing's for sure, he definitely had a way with words.

Restorative justice changed me. My eyes were sore, I was emotionally wrecked. But I had a new-found determination: I wanted to get my life back. And I intended to do exactly that.

I GUESS GOD THINKS
I'M ABEL

The smell of fried onions hit me. It was pure. Organic. An urban delight. It was Friday, market day. The town was heaving. People everywhere. I was smiling from ear to ear. I felt alive. I felt normal. For the first time.

I looked at Mr Byrd who was grinning at my happiness. I started playing with my wrists. It felt weird being in public without cuffs locked tight around them. As I was coming towards the end of my sentence, Governor Myers had agreed to let me have town visits. It's standard practice when you get close to the end of your sentence as a kid lifer. But not everyone gets approved. A lot of times it gets refused for security reasons and shit. But it was agreed for me, and I loved it.

I'd been given an extra six months on my sentence. Myers was right about the riot – he said it wouldn't go unpunished. I can't even remember what the six months was for exactly but, in the sum-up, it was a rundown of all the shit I'd caused. It was no shock. But my new-found good behaviour and co-operation with the restorative justice programme, held me in good stead. I never heard what Vic got but there were loads of rumours that he'd turned into a fucking maniac and that no prison could cope with him. Always wanted to know what happened to Apples, but never did. Raj started playing the game. Understood he had a long sentence for his happy slapping and, a bit like me, realised that you can only go against the grain for so long. Eventually you have to take a long, hard look at yourself.

The market traders yelled their special offers, the burger vans, cheap clothes, bootleg CDs, moody DVDs, the butcher's, the fishmonger's – wow! An early taste of freedom. Normality. Human beings rushed around, playing out their busy lives. I watched them. Listened to them. All too busy to appreciate the wonderful gift of freedom. But then, why would they? If you're not a criminal, why would you ever have your freedom taken away? But you never appreciate what you've got until it's gone. Fuck, I ain't preaching! But it's the little things that mean so much when you lose them.

And, for that reason, I walked at the speed of a snail.

Soaking up everything – loving every second of it.

'Come a long way from your early days in the Seg, huh?' Mr Byrd said.

'Shit, feels like a lifetime ago. I can't even believe I'm the same person.'

'You're not, son, believe me.'

'Was I that bad?' I asked.

'Cain, all the officers were worried when they had to work with you. You were always a big lad. But the problem was, you were a big lad with a stinking attitude. And a blinding left hook . . .' He grinned, rubbing the side of his face.

'I'm sorry about that, Guv. Dunno if I ever really said sorry properly.'

'Ha ha, you did.' He mimicked a young rude-boy, 'In a "yes, blood" way!'

I punched his arm playfully, laughing.

'We gotta go in there.' JJB Sports. It was my second town visit and, this time, I had some spends to get clothes and that – Emma had sorted it out for me. I ran inside. I went straight to the trainers. Never the practical stuff first. Running trainers. Asics. The best. I was running 10k in under thirty-five minutes. Which, if you don't know, is bloody fast. I was hooked. My feet were like hammer shit from running in prison-issue pumps. I spent ages just touching all the different trainers. Sounds silly but I sniffed at the brand new materials and they smelt amazing. I must have tried on a dozen pairs. Every fucking one in there. Mr Byrd was cool as fuck, though –

didn't rush me. Just let me get on with it. Once I'd picked a pair, Mr Byrd said, 'Let's get you some clothes, too. Otherwise you'll be staying celibate when you get released!'

He was a snappy dresser. Cool shoes, smart jeans and a Ralph Lauren jacket. All a bit posh for me. He was right, though, I needed some new clobber. We went around a few more shops and agreed to disagree on a lot of the fashion we saw. But, I must say, he did have some influence. It would have been tracksuit and baseball cap, end of, in the old days. We reached a compromise – smart jeans, black-and-white checked shirt (never worn a shirt in my life until that point), but with white trainers and a LA Lakers baseball cap. Smart, but sticking to my roots, yeah! A new Cain, but with some of my original tastes.

I got into my new kit and, as we walked around, I saw some girls about my age. They were pointing at me and giggling. I gave them a little wave. Polite and all that. It felt good. It felt nice not to be looked at like a piece of shit. It felt like I was actually being somebody. But the only girls I wanted to see were Lily and Lola. I pined for them both. Believe. I was more head-over-heels in love with Lily than ever before, if that was possible – even though I'd not seen or heard from her in a very long time. But I never gave up writing to her. I told her how I'd changed and that, when I got out, I would study hard and get a good job, and pay for our daughter and shit. I sent poems to both of them; I told her my fears, worries and excitement. Everything. Never got a reply. I don't know if she'd moved or not. Sometimes I was close to ringing the house, but the thought of rejection – or, worse still, to have it confirmed that she'd moved away and I'd never see her again – was too much to bear. I found it easier to post the letters and hope and pray that one day my dream of being reunited with them would be fulfilled.

Suddenly, I saw the golden arches. 'Guv, let's fucking eat, yeah?' Maccy-D's – heaven.

My tray was full to the brim with an assortment of burgers, fries, milkshakes, doughnuts, nuggets – the lot. I was ramming it down my neck like I'd never eaten before. Because of all the exercise I was doing, I was hungrier than usual. Story of my life. And the big M, damn, was always my favourite.

'You fucking pig!' Mr Byrd couldn't believe what he was witnessing.

'Best food in the world, Guv!'

I ploughed through every bit of grub on my tray and all the leftovers Mr Byrd couldn't finish. I was uncomfortably full. But I loved that feeling – your definition of uncomfortably full is my definition of well and truly satisfied. I sat back in my chair and took a deep sigh as I loosened my belt. I literally couldn't move. I lifted my crisp new cap and wiped my brow. I was hot. Mr Byrd was reading a newspaper. It was nice, just watching the day go by. I felt better than I ever remember feeling.

I loved to people watch. I slowly scanned the room. A middle-aged woman at the counter was looking around to see if anyone had noticed her extremely large order. She carried more meat than a lady of her height should. The way she pulled at her clothes told me she was uncomfortable about it, but still she ate shedloads of grub. There was a couple sitting near us; they must have been only a few years older than me. He was wearing a high-vis vest and workman boots; she cradled a little baby on her lap. He kept looking at his watch; he'd obviously snuck off to meet his young family. A well-dressed man in a pin-stripe suit and smart glasses smiled from ear to ear as he collected his food. Better than that poncy shit he's forced to eat with the other toffs, I bet. I chuckled to myself as I looked, enjoying each story that I imagined for the strangers around me. I continued to scan the room – a loner sitting at a table with a lap-top computer. Next to him were a couple of— Fuck. The loner. Shit, who was he? I quickly looked back; I half recognised him. I looked properly for a minute. All of a sudden I felt an electrifying stab go straight through my heart, with the pain speeding around my entire body. I felt lifeless. Vulnerable. Scared.

Eight years old and I'm asleep in my bed. Fast asleep. I'm woken by my pyjamas being ripped away from my body. In a disorientated daze, I try to get up, unaware of what is happening. I feel a blow to the back of my head and I'm forced down on to the bed. It's the noise of his belt being undone that will never leave me.

And there, in McDonald's on only my second town visit, Sick Boy was sitting alone, stuffing his face and looking at his lap-top. I felt raped all over again. Abused.

Violated. I started to shake, both my legs bobbed up and down like crazy. I looked at Mr Byrd; he was unaware of what I'd seen. Unaware of what was going through my mind. Unaware of the situation I was in.

The flashbacks fired through me, at a million miles an hour. His breath, his hands, his fat, stinking body. I shook. I bounced my legs. I clenched my fists. Fat cunt. Dirty, fat cunt. Horrible pig cunt. Raping scum cunt. A little boy with nothing and no one. A little boy with innocence and freedom; unaware of the sick realities of men. Raping, dirty, sick men. Animals. My life, my innocence ripped away from me. Stolen is not a strong enough word. Ripped away from me. By him – Sick Boy.

My fear started to turn into anger. Lust for blood. I clenched my fist and started fantasising about killing him. Ripping his liver out. Maiming him. Fat, spotty, dirty, sex-offending vermin. Bastard. Pig. I looked at him. Pathetic. Small. Chubby. Geeky. Nothing. I was powerful, see. Big and powerful. I'd developed my body as a machine. Fitness. My heart was strong, yeah. He has no fucking heart. The muscles that protected my body were strong. I could smash down a building. I could use it to move mountains. Sick Boy, he was nothing in comparison to me. I was a man. A strong man. I looked at him. He was so small, puny. The big terrorising cunt he used to be had disappeared. I could smash him, yeah, smash him. I could kill him. I've done it before. I'll kill him. Fucking pig.

I sat there, fantasising about going over and killing him. Not hurting or hitting him. But killing him. Getting that lap-top and forcing it up him, forcing it up his fat arse till he bled to death. I could do it. Strong, see. Powerful. I was a man; he was nothing. I was in control. I could do it. I knew I could do it. I was in control now, not that fucking bastard. I will show him, fucking animal. ME, I'M IN FUCKING CHARGE.

'Cain, you all right, son? You look really pale.' Mr Byrd was concerned.

'What?' I was shaking like a madman.

'What's wrong?' he asked.

'N . . . N . . . Nothing, Guv.'

He looked at me, worried. I continued to look at Sick Boy; he was just sitting there eating, getting fatter, looking at his screen. Mr Byrd looked at who I was looking at. He looked back at me. He evaluated the situation.

'We're going to get up, walk out of here and go to HMV,' he said in a calm, instructor's tone.

I shook my head. I had more important things I needed to do.

'Cain, look at me.' I didn't. 'LOOK AT ME.' I turned to face him. 'He's not worth it, OK, let's just get out of here.'

I looked up and tried to see the reason in his words but the flashbacks started again, 'It's him, it's fucking him! How can you say it's not worth it? I've told you what he done.'

'You don't need to do this; you're getting your life back.'

'Yeah, one that he fucking took away at eight years old.' I was getting animated. 'EIGHT FUCKING YEARS OLD.' People on the next table looked over.

'Keep your voice down,' he said. 'You do this, everything you've worked for, the whole lot, it's gone.'

He knew what I was contemplating. Not just hitting him, destroying him. He'd have to stop me; everything would be fucked. He knew, fuck, Byrd knew me too well.

'It's just . . . he fucking . . . How can I . . . ?'

'Cain, listen, mate, you are above this. Don't let him ruin your life all over again.' Then he spoke to himself, 'Fuck, what are the chances of this happening today.'

'Exactly, it's a chance to finish this. Let's go!' I jumped up from my chair and started walking towards him.

'Cain!' he yelled as he followed me.

I walked towards Sick Boy, not taking my eyes off him for a split second. Watching him eat. Watching him smile and laugh at whatever pervy images he had on his screen. I edged closer, staring at him the whole time. He'd not even noticed me. Too busy going about his business. I was practically on top of him and all he was doing was laughing. In his hysteria he knocked his mobile phone off the table on to the floor. It landed right by my feet. He looked at the phone and then his eyes followed my feet all the way up to my face. Mr Byrd stood back, knowing it was out of his hands now. This was my call. Our eyes met. I didn't say anything. Not a word. He just stared at me. Ill at ease, probably because of my size and the look in my eyes, but I'm pretty sure he didn't recognise me. The look I gave him went deep into the uncomfortable zone. Even if he didn't recognise me, he knew not to move. He knew that I was standing over him, that I was the one in charge.

He started to fidget uncontrollably, not really knowing what to do with himself. I moved at lightning speed as I crouched down to pick up his phone. I didn't take my eyes off him. I slowly clutched the phone in my hand and passed it to him. As he took it, his finger touched the back of my hand. I flinched, which made him jump. Then I took a deep breath and allowed him to take the phone. He took it with extreme caution. He knew. Bastard knew I was in control.

'Er . . . Thanks . . .' he mumbled.

'Word of warning – keep them hands to yourself, yeah? Because you never know who's just around the corner waiting for you.'

He stared at me confused and scared. He just froze. He was pathetic. Weak. One of life's inadequate scum. I stood up, not taking my eyes off him as I did so. I clenched my fist and bit my lip. I felt a lump growing in my throat. I squinted my eyes and thought about my future, not the life he'd taken away. I slowly began to walk for the door. I heard a sigh of relief as Mr Byrd followed. I looked around at Sick Boy; he looked back at me, two or three times. He knew. He fucking knew what I was saying.

I got outside and I walked three or four paces into a nearby alley. I turned and vomited everywhere. I was sick as a dog.

'You all right, son?' Mr Byrd asked.

Through spit and sick I said, 'Yeah . . . I did it, I fucking did it. That bastard has no control any more.' I spat out some more puke. The whole episode had a severe effect on my body. Sickness was the only way to get it out. I wiped my mouth and took a deep breath. I'd finished it. I was back in control. I chose what happened in there. Me. ME. I was in control. I felt liberated. I'd faced the real demon from my past and I came out the other side unscathed. I wanted to smash him. Hurt him. But walking away, not letting him ruin my life again, that was the biggest test of all – one that gave me a real chance to move on. And I had done it.

DOVES

I stared at my cereal bowl and waited. I never started eating until all the milk went chocolatey. I couldn't taste the chocolate properly until the milk had drawn out all the flavour. Coco Pops – love them. I put my spoon in and was about to load it up – then I stopped and waited for the milk to change colour completely. I was smiling to myself as I waited. I looked around and saw a dozen or so other boys getting their breakfast. Most of them looked tired; a lot of them limped around with rude-boy attitudes. I was different; I didn't feel like them any more. And it was the last day I was going to have to see them.

I was eighteen and a half – actually, it was getting close to my nineteenth birthday. It was the day of my release.

Even though I was over eighteen, I was still at The Well with all the other trainees. That's how it goes sometimes. At eighteen you should be moved to big-man jail. Prison goes in three stages: Juvenile is fifteen to eighteen; Young Offender is eighteen to twenty-one (and this is a Unit or Wing in big-man jail); and then when you're over twenty-one it's full-adult. I was still at The Well because I was so close to being released. The Youth Offending Team were sorting out my probation. Emma had been working with St Mungo's, a charity for the homeless, to help get me an approved place to live. All of that stuff needed to be sorted before my probation could be approved. And while all that happened, I had to carry on as normal. That's how it rolls.

Everything had finally been approved and my day had come. I was happier than ever because I'd also got a reply back from Lily. YES! She did live in the same place. Her dad had been stopping her mail for a really long time, but her mum couldn't take the deception any longer and had given her the letters. When she finally wrote back, she explained it all. She told me it took her a while to read all my stuff and then to make up her mind to write back. She was unsure, see? Didn't know whether I was genuine. Our daughter was two-and-a-half years old so she had to think of her first. She didn't know if introducing me into her life would be right for our daughter. I was a boy-turned-man who had been in prison for the last three-and-a-half years. She didn't know if I'd changed properly. I had written from the heart in all those letters, but the only person she knew was me on the outside – the homeless, junkie, fifteen-year-old boy.

So she started to write to me again, sending me pictures of her with Lola. I had them plastered all over my cell. I carried one with me the whole time. I couldn't send pictures back, for obvious reasons, so I used to draw for them instead. All sorts of pictures. I'd copy some, invent others – Lola was obsessed with the Tweenies so I'd draw them for her all the time.

I'd really found my love for drawing again. So much so, that I wanted to take it further. Actually learn about it. I'd been spending a lot of time over at education – I had been allowed to do art again. I had started to build up a decent portfolio of work. Along with exercise, art was pretty much the missing link that I had been looking for. A direction I felt that I wanted to go in. One of the conditions of my probation was that I either get a job or study. I said I wanted to do something with my artwork and my teacher fully supported me, saying that I did have a talent. With Emma's, Mr Byrd's and my art teacher's help, I applied for a full-time course doing a BTEC Introductory Diploma in Art and Design. I had never taken any GCSEs and I hadn't had any formal education but my literacy and maths weren't too bad. I was no Einstein, but I got by. I had to sit a few aptitude tests to make sure I was up to it – and I did this at the prison. I think I was a pretty unique case. I don't think they got many kid-to-man prisoners applying. I passed the tests and my portfolio impressed the college board and so it was agreed that, when I got out, all I had to do was go for an interview, so they could make sure I really wanted to do it – kind of like a job interview – and then I was in.

I was over the fucking moon, to say the least. Lily was talking to me, I had a place to go and live, I was almost accepted into a college to do art, I was close to being released and I would finally get to hold my daughter. I really felt like I was turning things around. My nightmares had subsided and I didn't feel like self-harming, ever. I was still a fitness fanatic; I didn't want to risk stopping in case they came back. But then, why should I? It's not as if it was an unhealthy habit.

I'd also exchanged a few letters with Mrs June. After our meeting she wrote to me. Not straight away. I think it was a few weeks, maybe a month, later. It was a very, very kind letter. You may think it's strange – her writing to the boy who killed her son. No stranger than I thought it was myself. But that day when we met face to face, there was a connection between us. Well, TJ was the connection. It was built on sadness – no, sorrow – a parental, caring, sorrow. And when she wrote to me, it was full of motivational encouragement; telling me not to waste my life, to try to turn things around and that I still had time to make something of myself. It really did move me. Her letter showed me that humans can change. And, ultimately, that humans can forgive. It took me a while to write back. I had more false starts than I care to admit. How do you start a letter like that? But I did it eventually, by simply thanking her. I couldn't say sorry again. I'd given her my apologies. And they were sincere. Any more and I would have been doing it for the wrong reasons. I totally regret what happened and what I did, but I wasn't the only guilty person in all of it. That was something I also had to accept. Once I'd taken responsibility for my actions, I had to learn to let go of the things that I wasn't in control of. She wrote to me again, asking me to stay in touch and to keep her updated with my progress. I guess, in a weird kind of way, keeping in touch with me reminded her of TJ. I'm not suggesting that I could replace her son. I'd never say shit like that. But perhaps it made her feel closer to him. I don't know. But I liked talking to her. I liked the way it made me feel. It made me feel settled and it helped me come to terms with everything.

I felt like I had purpose. An actual reason to be alive. And in Lily's last letter to me, she agreed to come to the prison on my day of release to meet me at the gate. I knew she wouldn't bring Lola – she didn't want her anywhere near the place. Plus, if I did turn out to be the person I was promising to be, she didn't want Lola to have any memory of me in prison, however distant it would be because of her age. That all made perfect sense. There was no promise of a romance, or anything. Just a promise to see how it went. Take things very slowly and if I did what I said I was going to do, then I'd get to see my daughter. I had everything to live for. Everything to motivate me to stay on the straight and narrow. I had a lot to look forward to. And I was still just eighteen years old.

I smiled and filled my spoon, knowing that this really was the first day of the rest of my life.

'What do you mean, you FUCKING PRICK? You ain't got a FUCKING CLUE, BLOOD.' I looked up to see some lad gobbing off at a screw.

I was still in prison for now.

'Who the fuck do you think you're talking to? I'm not your blood. It's Guv to you. Now back to your cell.'

'Fucking make me, you CUNT.' He swung a punch.

BANG! The screw dropped him to the deck in a flash. I'd seen it a million times. Had it done to me a million times. I was over it, big time.

Another screw hit the alarm bell. 'IN THE SHOWERS,' she ordered.

Normal procedure when someone has been bent up – everyone else has to be banged away. And you get put behind the nearest door, so they can clear the area and take the boy to the Seg as quickly as possible. The closest place to the dining hall was the showers.

Shit, my milk had just turned chocolatey, as well.

I felt really smart in what I was wearing. I had the clothes on that I had bought when I was last on a town visit with Mr Byrd. My jeans were faded blue, my trainers were plain white K-Swiss and my checked shirt looked even better than last time. My Lakers hat was bright yellow – the bollocks, mate. I'd had a shave and a good wash, too. I felt ready and nervous as I sat in reception waiting to be escorted to the gate for the final time.

I had a small bag with my belongings, which I held tightly in my lap as I watched the screws go about their business. The place is a factory, it just keeps on going. I saw one or two new arrivals wander in as I sat there. Some were nervous, others cocksure and full of attitude. Shit, I'd changed. Big time.

'No, I say how it is, not you – let's get that right from the start. This ain't school and I'm not a teacher. You're in prison and the rules stand. This ain't a democracy, you do what you're fucking told. Understand?' I half smiled as I listened to the screw's orders to the new arrival. In a weird way it reminded me of the journey I'd just taken.

I was excited and slightly scared about being free. Three-and-a-half years may not sound like a long time to some people for what I did. My crime was bad. But I've got a life sentence. Sure, I'm not spending it in prison, but I will never be able to get over the things I did as a stupid, drug-addicted kid. It's easy for the armchair judge to say, 'Three years is not long enough.' But three-and-a-half years in juvenile prison are not a walk in the park. It's not easy. It's fucking hell – I came close to death more than once, and considered suicide as a real option. My sentence didn't finish the day I was released – I killed a boy and I have to live with that for the rest of my life.

My guts were doing cartwheels. I was so nervous. Believe. Not just about being let out, although that did play a part, but the fact I was going to see Lily. Actually get to see her in the flesh for the first time in ages.

'You ready, mate?' Mr Byrd had walked over to collect

me. He had said he'd be there to walk me to the gate on my way out.

'You look knackered, Guv!' He had bed-head and seemed barely with it.

'I was out on the sauce last night,' he mimed having a drink. 'I don't start till one o'clock, but I came in early because I couldn't bear the thought of not seeing your ugly mug before you go!'

We both had a laugh. I got up, clutching my stuff, and had one last look round at the prison reception.

'Nah, blood, you ain't looking at me, you batty boy!' one of the lads said.

'Guv, not blood. You get strip searched in prison. It's not a request; it's an order, so move your arse.'

I chuckled to myself as Mr Byrd and I walked out of reception and on to the route for the final time. The Well, the crime, the time – it just keeps rolling on and on. It never stops.

There was a chill in the air as we walked along the route. I saw a couple of screws buzzing around, going from one location to the next, hardly even noticing anything, in their own little worlds. People watching – it's amazing. I started to shake a little from nerves and excitement. I couldn't wait to see Lily.

'She's coming to meet me today, Guv.'

'I know, you've told me a million times.' He smiled.

'It's amazing; I can't wait to see her. I'm really going to try, Guv, I'm gonna make something of myself.'

He stopped and looked at me, 'Don't let me down. Nah

– don't let yourself down, Cain. You've been through a shitload and you've come out the other side a changed person. That don't happen often. But at your age, every now and again it does. Shit, that's why I work here and not with adults. They're all fucked!' We both laughed.

'I ain't gonna fuck it up – got too much to live for. I'm gonna study and get a good job, yeah. Got a kid, innit. And Lily. Hopefully I'll have Lily as well.'

'Do it for yourself, too. Not just for everyone else.'

'I am doing it for myself. But, ya know, I also got other things to help motivate me.'

'As long as you do, mate. I've got a lot of faith in you. And that other thing. That . . . The one that . . . Him . . .' He struggled to spit the name out.

'Sick Boy?'

'Yeah. You know I really think you should make an official complaint to the Old Bill. You don't know what else he's been up to since. He's a fucking scumbag who should be locked up for what he did.' Mr Byrd had been trying to get me to make an official complaint since we'd seen him that day. I wasn't ready to do that. I didn't know if I had the strength to go through with it.

'I ain't, Guv. Don't think I could do it. Besides, I feel like I got some sort of closure that day.'

'Well, you know what I think. You never know what he's . . .'

I interrupted, 'I know what you think, Guv, and, like I said, I don't want to do anything about it right now.'

'Listen, lad, you ever change your mind and you want

someone to go to the police with you, you just ring the nick, ask for me and I will go with you.'

'Would you?' It was over and above.

'That's a promise, mate. Any time.' A good bloke.

We got to the gate house and stepped inside. I was minutes, no seconds, away from stepping out of that gate for the final time. As a free man. MAN. We walked through the gate where there were two officers working. I knew them both from my time spent inside. They waved and said, 'Good luck.'

I was really nervous. The excitement was doing me in.

'This is as far as I go, mate,' said Mr Byrd.

'What about Governor Myers, where is he? I wanted to say goodbye.'

'He wanted to be here, but he was, well . . .'

'Helping someone or something as usual.' I finished the sentence for him.

'Yeah, you know him,' he said. 'Look after yourself, Cain. This is your chance to go and make something of yourself. You're still a kid. Sorry, I don't mean that, but you're still young, you really have got a chance to go and get that life you've always dreamed about.'

'I will do, Boss.' I held out my fist to his, 'Safe, yeah?'

'Safe!' he said as we touched fists.

He joked around, wrestling with me and putting me in a headlock.

'Mind the cap, yeah, it's proper!'

He unlocked the door in front of me and let me out. We shook hands properly. Like one man with another.

'I'll be seeing you, yeah?' I said.

'Hopefully not, mate, in the nicest possible sense. Be lucky.'

I stepped out of the door and took a deep breath in through my nose. The deepest I think I've ever taken. The smell of freedom. You can't put a price on it. I looked back at Mr Byrd as he shut the door. He really is a geezer, no question about it. He's one of life's truly decent men. I hope I get to meet more like him.

I looked around for Lily. I looked left and right. I couldn't see her. I walked a few paces, then I saw Emma's car. Excellent. She said she'd be coming. Although I was over eighteen and didn't technically come under social services any more, she'd dealt with me for years and had been the one who helped me find a place to live and stuff, so she had arranged to see it through by picking me up and taking me to my new place. She was going to pick Lily up and bring her along with her. I saw the car about fifty metres away. I couldn't contain my excitement; I started running over to it. I had the biggest smile and, as the cold air hit my face, I ran like the wind. I was only a couple of metres away when Emma got out of the car. Emma. Only Emma. I stopped in my tracks and stared through the windows of the motor. I couldn't see anybody else. I looked again. She must be in there. It must be a joke.

'Ha ha, where is she?' I said, half laughing.

'She's not here, Cain.'

I walked around to the boot. 'She climbed in there

as a joke, didn't she?' I said. 'Lily, very funny, out you come!'

'She didn't come with me, Cain,' Emma said again.

'LILY,' I shouted, 'OUT YOU COME.'

'CAIN, LISTEN TO ME.' I looked at her. 'She's not here. She didn't come. She changed her mind at the last minute.'

As the words left her lips, it felt like I'd been stabbed in the heart. I felt like I could cry, vomit or collapse at any moment. I didn't, though. I just stood there in stunned silence. Everything I was dreaming of, the whole thing came crashing down. Who was I kidding? As much as I tried to keep my feet on the ground, I had still been hoping – praying – for a tearful reunion. Only this was real life, not the ending to a Hollywood movie. And it was real. Believe. Every part of my body felt it. I couldn't even bring myself to speak. I couldn't move. I felt paralysed, both physically and emotionally.

'She didn't think it was the right time for her to see you. She wasn't ready for it. She's unsure if, you know, this is all going to work out right for Lola,' Emma said.

'Fucking hell, Emma, she wasn't even bringing her – this was just a first meet, ya know? Where we could talk and shit. You are here and everything as well, so the pressure is off. It was going to be so perfect.'

'You have to see it from her point of view. You've just got out of prison. You have a daughter. She's seen you once in the last three-and-a-half years. It is a big step, even if it doesn't seem like it is that much of a big step to you.' I knew it was a big step, but I had romantic blinkers on.

I got into her car. I was so upset. I was hurt. Destroyed. I had been looking forward to seeing her so much.

Mr Byrd's words came back to me – I had to do it for myself, as well. I was. I'm not lying about that. But I realised that I had been pinning too much hope on the other stuff. Running before I could walk.

'I'll tell you what, there's a McDonald's Drive Thru a couple of miles away. How about we stop there and you can get some food? Do what you normally do and order the whole menu!'

'I'm not hungry. Let's just go, yeah.' And I wasn't. For the first time in my life the thought of eating actually made me feel sick. I was devastated.

It was a good two , maybe three-hour drive. I slept a lot of the way. I got the odd tap from Emma because of my snoring. Other than that, I just slept. Emotional exhaustion killed me. It was only after a tear up that I'd suffered this extreme tiredness before.

Emma tapped my arm, 'Wake up, sleepy head, we're nearly there.'

I peeled open my eyes. Although it was only mid-after-noon, it was pretty dark. The sky was deep grey and everywhere looked pretty damn miserable. It was a reflection of how I was feeling. That release day should have been the happiest day of my life. I'm not saying it was the saddest, but I was gutted by not seeing Lily.

I knew the town I was in – not that well, but I knew it. It was about a twenty-minute drive from where I used to live and, of course, where Lily and Lola lived. I didn't want to go back to the old town. But I also didn't want to be a million miles away from my daughter and Lily.

It was a big place – more like a city, really. The college and university were amazing. So everything was spot on. I felt really solemn, though. Like a cloud was hanging over me.

We pulled into an estate that was full of Victorian buildings. We stopped outside a great big terraced house. It was three-storeys high and had a basement. It looked old but the area didn't appear to be too bad. It was also walking distance from the town centre and college.

'Here we are!' Emma tried to sound as upbeat as she could.

I didn't say anything. I got out of the car and grabbed my stuff. I looked up at the building; it was huge. It had five massive steps leading to the front door. It was a steep climb. Emma was only short and it looked like she'd barely be able to lift her legs high enough. As I got closer, the front door burst open. Out walked a black geezer with gold teeth. Looked every bit the drug dealer. He had two mates with him, but they were a lot younger and full of attitude. The three of them stared at me as I walked up. Sizing me up. The two younger lads were giving it the most. They must have been fourteen or fifteen. I looked back, but didn't hold their stare. I didn't want any trouble. The place wasn't the Ritz after all. I don't know what I was expecting. I had just had a vision of something perfect in my head. Like a naïve idiot. Yeah, I'd come a long way but, fuck, I was nowhere near where I wanted and needed to be. I'd barely reached the starting line.

Emma unlocked the front door and I went in. There was a huge hallway and some stairs in front of me. The place stank of piss and was really dirty. Thick cobwebs hung from every corner. My room was the first on the right.

'Here we are, Cain, this is yours.'

She opened the door. A musty smell of death hit my nostrils. It was a pretty decent-sized room; that's the only thing it had going for it. It had hard-wood flooring caked in a thick, black grime – obviously not been cleaned for a long time. It had a sink with a broken mirror above it, a single bed that had seen better days and a small table and chair that needed a good wash. The table had a fourteen-inch TV sitting on top of it. The screen was cracked and it was covered in thick dust; I was pretty sure it wouldn't work.

'Where's the wardrobe for my gear?' I asked.

'It's not perfect, Cain,' she said, seeing my concern, 'but it's a start. A home is as nice as you want to make it.' I guess that was true. 'You've got to report to the Town Hall at nine fifteen tomorrow morning to sort out your benefits. Then you'll need to be back here for midday as your YOT worker is coming round to see you. Then it's off to the college for your three p.m. interview.'

'Shit, all that tomorrow?' I said.

'Your new life starts with a bang, huh? You need to get on top of everything. You need to sort your money, comply with your probation terms of release and get into college. Your course actually starts next week.' She pinched my arm, 'All exciting stuff, hey?'

I smiled at her. She was right. It should have been exciting. But the reality was a kick in the bollocks.

'Thanks, Emma. You really have been a great help. I know I've not always been the easiest boy to deal with. And I am happy, I just feel, well . . .'

'I know it must be a shock and you must feel let down by Lily. But this is your first day, OK?'

She always was kind to me. She did over and above what she had to.

We said our goodbyes and she left. As the door shut, I looked around my room. It wasn't much. No, it was pretty damn grotty. But it was mine. My first home that was all mine. I could either be a kid and wallow in self-pity, or I could do everything in my power to make something out of it. I went over to the sink to look for some cleaning products.

There was a narrow cupboard I hadn't noticed when we walked in. I opened it to see an old broom that had practically no brush left, a mop that looked rotten, some cleaning detergent, which appeared to be stagnant, and some polish with no spray top. And some rags that looked like a bacteria playground.

'FUCK,' I screamed, as the biggest, fuck-off spider I'd ever seen came running out. Hate spiders.

I watched it run away into a crack in the wall. That was good enough for me. Out of sight and all that. I rolled up my sleeves and pulled myself together. I got out the cleaning stuff. First thing I had to do was clean the cleaning materials. OK, so the day hadn't gone how I'd hoped. I was done in about Lily but I wasn't going to let it beat me. I was allowed to be upset. But I wasn't going to let it get the better of me. I realised that, in life, things don't always go the way we'd like them to. Fuck, I'd felt the harsh hand of reality on more than one occasion. I guess what defines a man is whether tragedy breaks or makes him. I was up to my knees in shit and I spent the whole night cleaning. I'd chosen the latter. I was not going to be defeated.

POWER TO THE PENCIL
AND BODY

I looked down at the pictures in front of me. I'd written a pretty mad story to go with it. When I used to draw Shark-Boy, I'd just do different scenes and stuff. I had a story in my head, but I never actually drew a storyboard or put in any words. I'd grown really close to that character, as crazy as that sounds. He was my escape when I was a kid but he kept coming back. I'd been drawing him for so long and, six months into my course, I'd really refined his detail and story. He had grown up with me.

I was studying comics – the different kinds of stories, how they are put together and that type of stuff. We'd also started looking at graphic novels. I'd never even heard of one of them before I started the course. They're proper books with a comic-book-style content. Amazing things. Love them. I started getting loads of them out of the library. I had dreams of turning Shark-Boy into one.

Part of our coursework was to have a go at creating, drawing and putting together a comic story. The mad thing was, I had all these ideas about Shark-Boy's back-story and life and stuff, but I'd never written one word about it. I thought I'd hate doing it, but actually I loved it. And now I was putting the finishing touches to the first comic strip I'd drawn and written. It was only two pages but it had a beginning, middle and an end. I looked down at the different frames, seeing my character going through his journey. I know it was short, but it was so amazing to me to have created the whole thing. The story, the drawings and all the dialogue. Quality.

It was coming near to the end of the lesson and I wanted my lecturer, Tom Pinter, to take a quick look before I left. He was an older fella, a real free-loving, laid-back artist. He reminded me a lot of Governor Myers – only Tom was even more laid-back. Any more and he'd be horizontal. He took a keen interest in me from day one. I found it easy to talk to him. He never made me feel ashamed about my past. He thought it made me a stronger person.

Don't get me wrong, I didn't shout it from the rooftops that I was an ex-con. Only those who had to know about it knew. I wanted a new beginning; I didn't want to go on about my past. I was friends with most of the people on my course. Not close. I kept myself to myself. Most of them went out on the piss in town and shagged about. I'm not knocking it, but I wasn't strong enough to have a drink and leave it. I was scared to go to a pub in case it led me back to doing bad shit. So, I kept my distance.

I didn't want to get close to anyone, either – except Lily and Lola. Even though I'd been out for six months and Lola's third birthday had come and gone, I'd still not seen either of them. I wrote to Lily to let her know my address and the college I was studying in. I told her my programme; I gave her my mobile number. I had bought myself a pay-as-you-go phone. I even told her about my part-time job. I'd started working at the campus gym. A job had come up and I practically begged for it. I told the manager all about my past and my passion for fitness and what it did for me. She was so impressed with my enthusiasm and determination to change she gave me the job, even though I had no fitness qualifications. She sent me on a couple of weekend courses and, bingo, I was working in the gym every minute I wasn't studying. I didn't get paid lots of money, or anything. It was only a little bit higher than minimum wage. But I LOVED it, and it was more money than I'd ever had. Legally. I gave gym inductions and wrote fitness programmes for members and things. I was simply over the moon. Except that I still hadn't heard from Lily.

I didn't harass her. I didn't ring the house or go there, even though it was only twenty minutes away. I kept some dignity. I sent presents to Lola, though. Nothing big, just some teddies, colouring books, sweets and the odd fiver or tenner that I'd earned. I wanted to show Lily that I'd changed. Or was changing. That I was actually living up to my promise. Sure, it wasn't as easy or romantic as I dreamed it would be; fucking hard work and tiring the whole time, more like. But it was still great and I felt alive. Like I was being somebody. And I would show her fucking dad.

I was still pissed off at the way he had spoken to me. Plus, I totally believed he was putting the spanner in the works every time Lily and I started getting on. As we used to take loads of drugs together, she had had an unplanned teenage pregnancy because of me and I had been banged up, I could see why her old man wouldn't be that happy about her getting involved with a lad like me again, even if I was different. But he was pompous, arrogant and so fucking patronising. I know not everyone can forgive, but I had a child with his daughter and there was nothing he could do about it. And I was making every effort to be somebody. I wanted him to know that as much as Lily. Not that I thought I owed him anything, or that I needed his approval – I just wanted him to know that this scumbag wasn't on the waste pile just yet. I was changing, so he could stick his vicious words up his fucking arse. I didn't go round or phone because I didn't want to be a nuisance and prove him right. But I bet he used the fact that I wasn't going round to say it was because I didn't give a fuck. That's the type of bloke he is. Patience had become my virtue. It had to be. When you're behind a locked door with only yourself and your thoughts for company, you don't have a choice. So I decided to have some self-control and wait. And hope.

I quickly finished colouring the final frame of my comic strip and took it up to Tom. 'Take a look. Am I on the right tracks?' I handed him the work.

He took it and stared at it for ages. I stood there like a right tool, while he just looked and looked. Just like Myers would have done. No sense of time. Did he think it was shit, or was it good? I couldn't tell from his face. He scratched his head while he flicked back and forth between the pages. Maybe I'd completely fucked it up.

'This is . . .' COME ON! 'Well, I'm not sure if that's the right way of putting it.' The right way of putting what, you bloody hippy!? 'It's, well, fucking fantastic, Cain. I love it. You have a real flair for this. Your other stuff is good, that's for sure. But this – comic art is right up your street. A bloody great character and brilliant little story – well done. Is it OK if I keep this to show to one of my colleagues?'

WOW! 'Of course, Guv – er, Tom. Sorry, force of habit.' Some are hard to kick.

He really liked it. I was chuffed to bits. I looked at my watch; the bell was going to go any minute. I had to get over to the gym to start my shift.

'Thanks for your words, Tom. I'm really pleased

you like it. Is it OK if I chip off now? Got a shift in the gym.'

'Mmm, sure, go.' He waved his hands as if to shoo me away. 'You've done plenty of work, so get away. And, Cain,' he said, looking up at me, 'well done.' I smiled from ear to ear as I legged it out of the classroom.

I walked out on to the gym floor wearing my uniform polo T-shirt and jogging bottoms. I'd bought an awesome pair of Asics to wear, too – the gym gave me an allowance for things like that, as it was part of my uniform, so I picked a really expensive pair. I was greeted with several hellos from the regular users. It may sound silly, but I had a real sense of pride wearing that uniform and having some sort of respect from them. I loved that job.

'Hi, Cain, when's the next kettlebell introductory class?' a regular named Jessica called over. She was also a student at college. She was a few years older than me and, yeah, she was fit. She always flirted and I'd be lying if I said I wasn't flattered – she was my type, but everything I wanted was twenty minutes away in the next town.

'If you pick up a programme at reception, it has all the classes in it. Just make sure you put your name down – the introductory class is always busy.' I was the only kettlebell instructor in the gym. It's an awesome bit of kit – like a cannonball with a handle. Although, I don't think Jessica was that interested in kettlebells.

'OK.' I went to walk off. 'Er, Cain . . .' I stopped and

looked, 'a few of the girls and I are going to O'Neill's for a few drinks tonight. There's a good band on.' She started to look shy. 'We wondered if you fancied coming along and joining us.'

'Me and a group of girls, you crazy!?' I was pulling her leg, she laughed. 'I'm working here till nine, so I'll have to give it a miss.'

'Come down when you finish, don't think the band are even on until about ten.' She was really sweet.

'I really can't, you know, I've got a lot of coursework to do when I get home. You have a good night, though, yeah?'

'Sure I can't tempt you?' If things were different . . .

'Sorry, I really can't tonight. Have a good one.' I was as polite as I could be.

I went over to the middle of the gym, where the instructors' desk was. I pulled my mobile out of my pocket, put it on silent and laid it on the desk. The gym was pretty quiet. I had to do an induction an hour or so later but I was pretty free until then. If any of the gym users needed some advice or had any questions, I was there for them. I took a swig from my bottle of water and sat in a daydream.

'Cain?' I looked around.

There were two squaddies dressed in full kit – beret and all. They looked smart and fit. I looked them both up and down. It took me a while but I recognised one of them. 'Radman? Fuck, how you doing, bruv!?' He was smiling from ear to ear.

'Radman, who the fuck is Radman?' said the other fella, taking the piss.

He looked a little embarrassed. 'It's a nickname I used to have.' He looked at me. 'I'm just Si, now.'

'What? Shit . . . How've you been? What you doing here?' I was really excited to see him. He looked really well.

'I'm good, bruv. Been in nearly four-and-a-half years.' He showed me the tape on his arm. 'I'm a Lance Corporal now.'

I did a mock salute, 'Look at you, Boss!' He smiled.

'You're looking fit as fuck, Cain. You look like a different fella. You should think about joining up.'

'Don't think they take ex-cons,' I said. 'You heard I went down, yeah?'

'Yeah, I heard, mate. I still pop back to town every now and then. There's another lad in my platoon who's from there. A bit older, like. Heard that TJ and you had . . .' He couldn't find the words.

'It was bad, man. Proper. Ain't a day goes by that I don't . . .' I got a little defensive, 'It weren't all my fault.'

'I know, I know.' He moved on, 'You seem to be doing well now, though?'

'Been out six months; loving college, got a nice little number here. Things are good.'

'Where you living?' he asked.

'Got a bedsit just off the Maldon Road. Was a complete shithole when I moved in, but I'm slowly doing it up. Saving the pennies and all that. How's the army, then?

Can't believe how different you look.' Which he did. He looked like a proper man. Confident. Strong.

'Done two tours of Afghanistan, one of Iraq and been on secondment to Germany. Been out the country more than I've been in it.'

'That a good or bad thing?' I asked.

'Good, man. Shit,' he said proudly, 'better than all the crap we used to get up to.' He backtracked, 'Not that it was all bad.'

'I know what you mean, we had some laughs . . .'

'Yeah, we did,' he agreed, smiling.

'But some proper shit, too.'

We were both quiet for a moment.

'You off the, ya know?' he was a little apprehensive as he asked.

'I'm clean. Don't drink or nothing. Don't know if I ever will, ya know. Just working hard, keeping fit. After being banged up, I've got a different perspective. That and Lily. We've . . .' I didn't want to get into that. 'So, what you doing here?'

'We came to give a talk about life in the army. Career prospects and stuff. It's in the conference suite in forty-five minutes.'

'Why you in the gym?' I asked.

'Well, I'd heard you were out and shit, and at a college.' That didn't really answer the question.

'But how did you know I was here?'

'I was back at the old town yesterday,' he looked uncomfortable, 'and I bumped into Lily. She told me.' Just hearing her name and hearing that someone else had seen her made my heart sink. He must have known. I felt embarrassed that I didn't even get post from her.

'Oh right,' I said defiantly. 'She all right, was she?'

'Yeah, looked well. She's changed a lot.'

'Oh right.' I tried to seem disinterested.

'She was with Lou.'

'Lou?'

'Her daughter,' he coughed, 'your daughter.'

'Lola. Her name's Lola.' I bit my lip.

'Fucking hell, Si. Look at the arse on that!' Si's mate had just noticed Jessica.

'Give us five minutes, yeah?' Si said to his mate.

He nodded and floated off, not taking his eyes off Jessica the whole time.

'Your girl's beautiful, mate, she really is.' He was really sincere.

'I've got pictures of her. I send her presents and stuff, money as well when I've got it.' I wanted him to know that I wasn't a scumbag who shirked my responsibilities. I was far from that.

'I know, I know – she told me.' He really did have a maturity about him. He was older than me but it was also his way – he had a sense of leadership. He was stronger. Better for it.

'I've never seen Lola in person. Not even seen Lily since I've been out. I won't go back to the old town. Worried about who I might bump into. At least here it's a big enough town to blend in. A fresh start. Even though I can't see them, at least I'm not a million miles away either.' I used to persuade myself of that every day.

'I didn't speak to her for long, but she did say she was confused by it all. Worried that, Lou . . .'

'Lola,' I snapped.

'Sorry, Lola would be messed up by it. She's worried that you might slip back into your old ways.'

'Fucking hell, what do I have to do?' I was a little angry. 'I'm working my nuts off in college; I work fucking hard here. I don't go out, hardly ever, and if I do it's only to the cinema or bowling or something. I send her things. What else do I have to do?'

'I know, I know. If I'm honest, I didn't believe that you were in college doing art, working in a gym and a fitness fanatic. I would never have believed it unless I'd seen it with my own eyes. I just remember a Maccy-D-eating maniac who was always wrecked!' he said the last bit in jest. We both smiled.

'Still love the Maccy-D's, bruv!'

'Well, whatever your training regime is, stick to it cos you look hench.' A nice compliment.

'So do you, bruv,' I returned the praise.

'It's my job, I have to.'

I replied quickly, 'It's *my* job, *I* have to.' I looked down at the emblem on my work T-shirt and stood proud.

'Yep, I guess you're right.' He smiled, 'Like I said, it's a difficult image to muster, thinking of you doing all this and looking the way you do. It's hard for her. Plus, I reckon her old man gives her shit about it.'

'Muster!? What kind of word is muster!? Fuck, you really are a squaddie!' We pissed ourselves like old times. 'I reckon her dad is a big factor,' I agreed.

'Yeah. All I'll say is, don't give up on it. And, without sounding like a twat, well done for what you're doing. It's fucking great. I've never seen you look better.'

'Cheers, Rad . . .' I stopped and corrected myself, 'Cheers, Si.' We touched fists.

'It is really good to see you, mate. Let's keep in touch. I gotta get to this talk now, so I'll chip off.'

We exchanged e-mail addresses and phone numbers. He called his mate who was drooling over Jessica's backside as she pumped the cross-trainer and they left. I felt really good after seeing him. He was always switched on. He took his opportunity and got out early. Wise lad.

As they left I looked at Jessica working out. Yep, she really was hot! I grabbed my water and took another gulp. I checked my watch; I had a bit of time before my gym induction. I decided to have a quick workout myself. I turned the music up; the controls were at my desk. As I did so, I noticed '1 message received' on the screen of my mobile. I picked it up and hit the read button:

'It's Lily, this is my num. Sorry 4 not replying 2 u, lots going on in my head. Worried n stuff. Saw Si, got me thinking bout u. Thank u 4 gifts. Lola luvs them. Do u wanna meet in Costa tom bout 3? I'm in your town. Understand if not. I am proud of u, Cain. Xxx'

I read it over and over and over. Si had obviously said some encouraging stuff when he saw her. Leadership.

Wise. A top geezer. I was just pleased I had some credit left on my phone to reply. I couldn't believe it. I was so happy. Patience is more than a virtue. Believe.

L-O-L-A, LOLA

I was shaking my leg and I felt really alert. Caffeine wired. Costa was rammed. I was queuing up to buy my third large latte. I was going for decaf this time. I was getting the jitters. I'd never been in a Costa before, let alone had a latte. Didn't know what one was. Made from milk, so that was good enough for me.

It was nearly half three and still no sign of Lily. I'd sent her a couple of text messages. No reply. I refused to go, though. I couldn't believe she would stand me up. AGAIN.

'Two large decaf lattes, please.' I'd ordered Lily one each time, as well. As I drank mine, hers went cold. So I ordered her another along with mine, hoping she'd turn up to drink it this time. And the place was bloody expensive. Could have got a meal and a double cheese-burger at Maccy-D's for the same price.

The bloke who worked there looked over my shoulder to see two mugs, full and cold, sitting on the table just behind me. 'She's coming in a minute, see. She's running a bit late. She hates cold coffee.' He gave me a strange smile.

Funny thing was, I didn't know what Lily liked. It had been so long. And the first time around, we didn't spend much time doing anything other than getting mashed and having sex.

I collected my drinks on yet another small tray and walked back to my table. The place was heaving. I had to stop every pace or so, to try not to bump into someone. Just as I got near my table a couple sat down at it, even though I'd left my coat there to show it was taken.

I addressed the bloke, he was in his late twenties, 'Sorry mate, I was sitting there.'

'Didn't see your name on it.' Rude bastard.

'That's my coat on the . . .' I looked and saw he'd pushed it on the floor. 'Well, it was on the back of the chair. It must have fallen off.' He gave me a shit-eating grin. He knew that I knew he'd done it.

'You'll have to go and find another seat, we're here now,' he said flippantly.

'Listen, mate . . .'

'I ain't your mate, fuck off,' he barked.

I slammed my tray down, spilling some of the drinks.

'Listen to me. I was here first. I got someone coming to see me and YOU AIN'T FUCKING IT UP, so get out of my seat, yeah?' If he thought I was going to walk off with my tail between my legs just because I was younger and he was a lump, he'd picked the wrong bloke on the wrong day. He looked at me aggressively. I didn't take my eyes off him. Not even to blink. He realised I wasn't fucking about.

'Come on, John, there'll be another seat in a minute,' his missus said, realising her fella was being a prick. It also gave him a get-out card, so he could save face. He stood up, trying to laugh it off, as if he'd made the choice. Wanker. Bully.

I stared at him until he was out of my space and then I sat down. I hadn't spilt too much. The other two cups of cold latte were crowding the small, round table.

'Excuse me, love, can you take these and give the table a quick wipe, please?'

'Sure, no problem,' one of the waitresses answered.

She cleaned the table and took away the other cups. I put one cup in front of the other seat and one in front of me. I picked up my jacket, brushed it off and stuck it on the back of my chair. I gave myself the once over, making sure my T-shirt didn't have any coffee on it. I had smart jeans and my best trainers on, too. I'd shaved my hair, nice and neat, and shaped my stubble into a pencil-thin beard. Looked proper. Plus, I'd got a fake diamond stud that I had in my pierced, left ear. 'It's all fine, you look good,' I told myself. The only thing that was doing me in was Lily – where was she?

'Hi, Cain.'

I froze for a second. I recognised that voice. I swallowed hard and took a deep breath. I looked around and Lily was standing over me. Her hair was a beautiful, rich brown, dead straight and it looked immaculate. She had subtle make-up, business-like and pretty. That's when I noticed she was wearing a suit. My chin hit the floor, she looked so gorgeous. I jumped out of my chair to greet her.

'Lily!' I went to hug her, but stopped. I didn't know what to do. So I put my hand out to shake hers.

'Come here, you dummy!' she said, leaning forward. We kissed each other's cheeks. As she did, she put one of her hands on my chest.

'Blimey, you have been working out, haven't ya?' She looked me up and down.

I really did look different. Not a lanky, emaciated hoodie. I was muscular, toned and in the best shape of my life. I'd never looked after myself so well.

I smiled, 'Realised you only get one of these,' I pointed at my body, 'so thought it best if I started looking after it.'

'And haven't you just. Love the stud – suits ya. And the beard.'

'Enough, I'll start blushing!' Things were going better than I had hoped. 'Here, sit down. I got you one of them milky coffees.'

She smiled, 'Hang on a sec, can you make some room for the pram.'

Shit, I hadn't even noticed.

It was behind her, she pulled at it to manoeuvre it around the busy place. She was cool as, I couldn't believe it. She'd brought Lola. My daughter. Our daughter. My leg started to shake, my heart pumped.

'Don't just stand there,' she said, smiling, 'move that other chair out the way so I can get the pram in!'

'Right, er, OK.'

I grabbed the third chair at our small table and slung it out of the way. She turned the pram around as best she could. It was a tight space. Everybody was practically sitting on top of each other. She managed to squeeze it round and tuck it tight into the third chair's place. And there she was. Lola. In front of me for the very first time. She looked so big! She was three years old. She was wearing a frilly shirt and little cord trousers. Her hair . . . It was as rich as her mother's, only Lola's was in perfect little ringlets. She hadn't looked up yet. She had crumbs all down her front, along with a half-eaten biscuit. She was holding on to a teddy with a chewed ear and another plastic toy with all her might. I looked down at her, utterly speechless. She finally looked up at me. Her eyes were a deep green. She nearly knocked me over, she was so pretty. She was humming something and, as our eyes met, she gave me the sweetest and most innocent smile.

'Say hello, Lola. This is, Cain, the man who has sent you all those presents.'

'Hell-ow,' she said.

'And what do you say for the presents?'

'Fank ye-oo.' My heart nearly broke into a thousand pieces.

I looked at Lola and smiled. Then I looked at Lily, who was smiling proudly at our daughter. I couldn't believe it. A world away from who we both used to be. A different existence. Lily sat down. I just stood there staring at Lola. My daughter. My flesh and blood.

'Aren't you going to sit down, then? You had enough dramas trying to keep this table.'

Shit, she had seen the argument, 'It weren't like that, honestly, I didn't pick a row. He . . .'

She jumped in, 'All right, all right, calm down! I saw. The bloke was a complete tosser.'

Phew. 'I didn't want you to think I was trouble making. I'm not like that any more, see. Like I've been telling you in all my letters,' I was gabbling nervously.

'Forget it, Cain! I don't expect you to be some pushover or anything. The bloke was out of order and you dealt with it. Finished.'

'Good. It's just the first time you've seen me in years and I'm having a row with someone. I'm like, shit, I really have changed!' I put my hands up and laughed. She smiled.

'Careful of the language around Lola, she's got this way of copying words – especially swear words!'

I hadn't even thought about that. 'Sorry, I'll watch my Ps and Qs. Not been around many toddlers before.'

'That's OK,' she said, 'just letting you know.' She was really relaxed.

Lola sat contentedly, playing with her teddy and her toy. She wasn't paying any attention to us. We both took a sip of our coffees.

'If someone had told me that you'd be sitting in Costa sipping a coffee a few years ago, I'd never have believed it!' Lily said, smiling.

'Likewise! I'm not the only one who's changed.' And that was the truth. We both smiled and took another sip.

'Didn't think you were coming. I was getting worried.'

'Sorry about that, I wanted to call to say I was running late, but the battery on my phone went flat.'

'That's why you didn't reply to my texts.' I put my hands up, 'Not that I was stalking you or anything!' I was struggling to be relaxed.

'Cain, bloody hell, calm down will you.'

'Language!' I said jokingly.

'Look,' she had a more serious expression on her face, 'I'm sorry it's taken me so long to see you. I've not meant to mess you around. It just, well, it's been really difficult. After everything we went through. And now with Lola . . . I've had to put her first, ya know. She's the most important thing to me. Nothing else.'

'I know. I understand that, I really do. That's why I've not hassled you. Well, I've written you like a million letters but I figured you could just bin them if you didn't want them . . .'

'No, I loved them. I really do.' She looked deep into my eyes.

'Er . . . well,' I carried on nervously, 'I figured they wouldn't be, like, hassling you too much. But phoning or turning up, that would be one step too far.' I tried to contain my anger, 'And it would have pissed your dad off.'

She looked down, embarrassed, 'I'm sorry about him. I know he can be rude and stuff. But he is my dad and he's got my best interests at heart.' Yeah, but he's a prick.

'Fair enough. But he was, can't explain it,' I could easily but I chose to try and find kinder words, 'he's just, well . . .'

'An arrogant, patronising pig?' she finished my sentence for me.

I smiled. 'Something like that!'

'He's far from perfect and rubs people up the wrong way. But, like I said, Lola and I are always in the forefront of his mind. He just wants what's best for us.'

'What about hiding the letters? That was one step too far in my book.' I was starting to relax a little, but still couldn't let go completely.

'Yeah, he should have given them to me. It was my choice to make, not his. But he was just protecting his little girl, you know. Even so, I was confused, Cain. I didn't know if you were chatting bull. I'd been clean for a long time – sorted my life out and left all that other stuff way behind me. I didn't want Lola or me dragged backwards.'

'And I would have done that, would I?' I said defensively.

'That's the point – I didn't know. I still . . .'

'Come on, Lil, give me some credit. Even if it's just for today.' I had to defend myself to a degree.

She took another sip of her drink, 'OK, I'm just explaining it from my point of view; trying to make you understand.'

'I'm not saying it's been easy for you, but you gotta understand it's been hell for me, too. I've been in nick for years, after all that shit. I've never had nothing or nobody. I know it wasn't the most romantic story, you and me, and it was mega destructive back then – but you were the only person I really cared about. Even if we were kids. Then when you came to see me to tell me about,' I nodded to Lola, 'it changed my life. It was a shock, yeah, but it did have a decent effect on me. We were chatting and sh . . . sorry, stuff and then – Bam! It all stopped. It killed me, Lil. Killed me. I felt like you just wanted to rub my face in it.'

'It wasn't like that,' she snapped.

'I know, but when you're in a cell with nothing else to think about, it's hard not to think bad stuff. I'm not trying to play the victim here, just want you to know that it's not been a bed of roses for me either.'

We both had a breather and watched Lola playing. So cute.

I carried on, 'Then on my release day . . .'

'OK, OK, I get the picture.' She'd heard enough and I'd said my piece.

'So why are you dressed so smartly?' I changed the subject.

'It's for my job. I'm a trainee manager at Marks and Spencer, just around the corner from here.' In the same town as me?

'Here? For how long?'

'A couple of months.'

'A couple of months and I've not seen you?'

'It's a pretty big town.'

'How could you come here and . . . ?' I thought better of carrying on. It's about what's happening now, not the past. 'Sorry. How did you get that then?'

'After I finished college, I got good grades, applied, went through the whole interview process and got the job.' She always was mega switched on.

'That's quality. Bet the money is damn good?'

'Yeah, pretty good for my age. But it's the career prospects – pension, sick pay and promotion. It's all there.' Not many think of that when they leave college. Her old man being wealthy would have certainly influenced her to look out for that type of thing. And that I commend him for.

'What about Lola?' I asked.

'She goes to Sunshine's, a nursery just around the corner, three times a week and mum has her twice a week.'

I couldn't believe how close they'd both been for the last three months. I used to walk through town every day, going to college and stuff. Never seen them. Like she said, it was a fairly big town so it was easy to go unnoticed. Especially if you don't know someone's there.

'Can't believe we ain't bumped into each other,' I said. Instead of getting moody, I wanted to think positively. Yesterday I didn't have a hope of even seeing them.

'We're here to see you now, aren't we?'

'How comes you got Lola with you, then? Thought you wanted to check me out first?' I asked.

'Well, you were so persistent with writing to me. Like you said, you didn't hassle me. And then when I saw Simon yesterday, he just said one or two things about people changing and how, even if they haven't, there's no harm in taking a look then walking away if necessary. I guess he's seen some stuff in the army. So I just thought, what the hell? I'll come meet you. I had some holiday to take, so I thought I'd take the afternoon off and come see you. But then something came up at work so I had to stay a little longer . . . that's why I was late.'

'Comes with being a manager, I guess,' I teased.

'Trainee,' she said smiling, pointing to her M&S badge still on her suit.

'I hope I've not disappointed you?' I had to ask.

'Not at all. I'm so pleased I came. I could hardly recognise you when I walked in.'

'Er, I'll take that as a compliment.'

'It was meant as one.' She smiled and finished her coffee.

'So, can I see you again?'

She looked a little uncomfortable.

'What? Have I done something wrong?' I asked.

'No, nothing like that. It's just . . . Well, it's just . . .'

'What?' I asked.

'I'm seeing someone. It's nothing serious, but I thought I'd better tell you now rather than later.'

Gutted is an understatement. Reality punch in the boat. Did I really expect her to wait for me?

I felt a lump in my throat, but battled on, 'Oh well, that doesn't matter. As long as I can, ya know, be mates with ya,' I looked at Lola and ruffled her hair, 'and see this little tiger again, that's all that matters.' Lily's eyes started to fill up. 'You OK?'

'Yeah, eyelash.' She looked down and wiped her eyes with a serviette.

Lola began to wriggle; she wanted to get out of the chair.

'You can get her out, if you like. Have a quick cuddle.'

'Really?' She nodded for me to carry on.

I undid the reins of Lola's seat. As I did, she opened her arms and reached for me so I could pick her up. Her green eyes. WOW! She was so beautiful. I kissed her on the cheek. It came so naturally. I did it without even thinking about it. I sat her on my knee and felt like the proudest man in the world. Lily got her out some colouring stuff and Lola got to work straight away.

'She likes art, like me,' I said to Lily, over Lola's shoulder.

'She likes a lot of things like you,' she gave me a deep smile.

I helped my daughter colour and loved every second. Lily looked on with sad and emotional eyes. I was gutted she was seeing someone else. Life isn't perfect. But this was my first step towards being a father. All I wanted was to have a family. And now I did.

HISTORY (THE
BUTCHER'S REPEAT)

I don't know what it is, but I've always loved the smell of petrol. Love it. It's one of those smells that you can taste and gives you a headache. I took deep breaths through my nose as I filled up the car. I wanted to put a full tank in.

'You sure you don't want some money for this?' Lily shouted through the window.

'No, I told you, it's on me. You always drive me about.'

Lily had a really nice, new Vauxhall Astra. Air-con, multi-play and all the extras. It was great for Lola, being four-door and having a big boot. I looked through the window and pulled a silly face at her, which made her chuckle.

Lily really was doing well for herself. She was flying in her job. Within six months she'd started covering for managers in different departments. She'd be running her own department in no time.

I was coming to the end of my one-year course. I'd already done enough to get on to the two-year higher one. I was chuffed. Tom had backed me. My story fascinated him and, when there was no one in earshot, he'd get me to tell him stories from my life – and, in particular, prison. I found myself getting over-animated when I told him about it. I loved hooking him in as I told my war stories. I wish I could say I exaggerated a lot but, where I was concerned, the truth was more interesting than any fiction could have been.

I finished filling up the car and went into the station to pay. I looked back at Lily and Lola squashed up against the windows, pulling silly faces at me. I laughed and pulled one back. Lily then blew me a kiss.

Since our first meeting in Costa, Lily had been excellent about letting me see Lola. I'd meet up with them both at least twice a week. And it wasn't long before Lily was spending more and more time with me. It was perfect. M&S was five minutes away from my bedsit and college. I could meet her all the time for breaks and lunch. Sunshine's was only around the corner, too. I was introduced to the staff there as Lola's dad – but not before Lola was told who I was. She started calling me Daddy straight away. She just said, 'OK, Daddy,' when we told her, and she carried on colouring. It just fell into place.

Lily's bloke lasted about five seconds. I think by our third or fourth meet it had fizzled out with him. Not saying I'm Brad Pitt or anything, but I'm damn sure I was something to do with what happened. It really did feel like we were a family at last. We were both such different people. Totally different. Learned. Aged. Better.

I got back into the passenger seat.

'You really didn't need to do that, ya know.'

'Do what? I only paid for the fuel, Lil, bloody hell! You run me around all the time, it's the least I can do.'

'Thank you, sweetie. We should think about getting you some lessons; then you can drive this, too.' I loved it when she spoke long term. Made me so happy, like this was going to last forever. I was twenty years old and I felt like I had everything I'd ever wanted. Yeah, for my age I guess things were pretty serious. There weren't many people who had kids when they were nineteen. No, that's wrong. There weren't many people of my age with kids who were also in a stable relationship. It had taken Lily and me a long time and we had gone through a lot of shit to get to where we were, but we'd made it. OK, we'd been through more than most relationships but people who say their relationship hasn't got some baggage are lying.

'Why do I need lessons when I got my own personal chauffeur?' She hit me playfully as we pulled out of the station. 'Especially since my chauffeur is absolutely fucking hot!'

'Cain, language!' She couldn't help smiling as she said it.

We were at a service station about ten minutes away from the old town. I'd still not been back. I didn't need to. Didn't want to. Too many horrible memories about things that I used to get up to that I just didn't want to think about. Lily was good about it. She knew I didn't want to go back and she completely understood. We'd been to a nearby village to feed the ducks – Lola loved it. They both used to get annoyed with me because I'd eat most of the bread. Always hungry. They were both coming to stay at mine but Lily had forgotten to bring Lola's stuff with her. She'd offered to take me home before she went back to collect it, even though the village we were in happened to be closer to the old town than it did to where I lived. I didn't want to go back but she'd come all the way to pick me up before we went out, so I wasn't having her drop me off and then go all that way further, just because I couldn't sit in the bloody car.

As we got closer to the town, I fell into deep thought. It was hard not to. I'd not been that way for such a long time. The memories came flooding back. I had a little smile as I thought about Radman, me and TJ riding on our BMXs, trying to do tricks. I was always pretty crap at them. Yeah, there were some normal memories of childhood fun. Not many, but some. And they were the ones that first came to me. As we got closer, though, my memories started to change. Drugs. The need for gear. The desperate feeling I used to have flooding through my body. I felt pins and needles rush over me. I looked at Lily singing along to the radio, smiling. As I stared, she morphed into the old her – just for a moment. The gobby, trashy, drug-taking sket. Shit. What was I thinking? TJ. Shit. The fear of him. The drugs. Fuck, the drugs. Wasted. Hammered. Scared. Violent. I was walking around waiting for that fool to come for me. I ain't having that. Never. I'll show him. I had the weapon. Fuck. How did it lead to that? I was starting to fidget in my seat as the memories – fucking nightmares – came flooding back. We'd got into the town and I saw the street corners where I used to hang around. Fuck. I felt ill. It was worse than I thought it would be. The robbing, the fighting, the maiming. Shit, I felt like I was going to pass out. Why didn't I get her to take me home? I undid my window. I needed some fresh air.

'You all right, darling?' she asked. No I wasn't. I felt terrible. Bad. Scared.

'Fine, babe, just hot that's all.' Fuck, I felt terrible.

I felt some drool run down the side of my mouth; sicky saliva was trying to climb up my throat. Hold it down, son, come on, you can get through this. The fresh air hitting my face started to ease the pain a little.

She stroked my shoulder. 'Nearly there, won't be long now then we'll be going home, OK?' There was no hiding it from her. She knew me too well.

'Sweet, babe. I'll be fine. Just difficult, ya know?'

'I know,' she answered caringly.

As the town was only small, it wasn't long before we pulled into Lily's estate. That was a mad feeling, too. My smack dealer used to live on that estate. And another feeling, funny as it sounds, was one of escape – happiness. As much as Lily and I got up to no good together, she was my solace. Everything that made me happy. It was my respite from living on the street, robbing, stealing and causing havoc. Most of the things we'd done were bad, but I still remembered them with fondness. I loved her from day one. I ain't even lying. True romance.

Then the next thought popped into my mind, 'Is your old man going to be home?' I asked. She knew I didn't like him, and he didn't like me.

'Don't think so, doesn't matter if he is. You can wait in the car; I'll only be a minute.'

Lily had told her mum that we were a couple straightaway. She was fine with it. And Lily didn't take as long as you'd think to tell her dad. I guess all the shit we'd been through and stuff; she didn't see the point in lying. He wasn't happy, as you can imagine. Fucking hated it. I got some abusive phone calls to start with but I just ignored them. I was tempted to be a prick to him, treat him the way he treated me, but I rose above it. I didn't want to do anything that would piss Lily off. I used to fantasise about having it out with him, which was enough to give me some sort of satisfaction. I'd seen both of her parents a couple of times near M&S, back in my home town – they were both fine with me. Her more than him. She was really nice. He was frosty, on the brink of rudeness, but he managed to keep his tongue between his teeth, as did I, so it was OK. This time, though, I was heading to their house, which was their territory, so I hoped he wouldn't be in.

Lily parked the car on the driveway; I'd forgotten how impressive the place was.

'Right, I won't be a minute. OK?'

'His car ain't here, which is a good sign.'

She smiled and turned to Lola, 'Won't be a second sweetheart, OK? Be good for Daddy.' She touched her little nose and got out of the car.

Lily ran into the house. I sat there and looked around. I was pleased I had come – it was bad and I felt bloody ill for a second, but I got through it. I had made it back and was OK.

'Daddy?' Lola asked.

'Yes, darling?'

'I'm hungry.'

'How about we stop at Maccy-D's and you can have a Happy Meal?' I didn't fill her full of crap that often. Just as a treat.

'Yay!' she said.

'We better be extra nice to Mummy when she comes out, then, so she lets us stop on the way home.' She smiled at me cheekily.

Lily was coming out of the house in no time. I saw her turn and talk to someone at the door. She pushed the person and said, 'Just leave it.'

But his car wasn't there?

She came walking over to the car with a worried look on her face. Five seconds later, just before she could get in, her dad came walking out. Fuck.

'Dad, just leave it.'

Here we go.

'What? I've come out to say hello, that's all,' he said. I doubted it was that simple. I stepped out of the car. 'I just wanted to come out and say hello, Cain.' This time he spoke directly to me.

What was he up to? 'Hello,' I said back. It sounded a little rude, but I didn't mean for it to.

'How's college and the job?' he asked. He'd never paid any interest before.

'Both great, thank you.' I didn't return questions to him. I was extremely cautious.

'I hear you've got on to the higher course. Well done,' he tried to sound enthusiastic but it came out a little flat.

'Thanks.' I had no idea where this was heading.

He could sense my caution. 'Look, I just wanted to come out here and say hello. I'm not going to lie to you; I've hated the idea of you two being back together . . .'

Lily interrupted, 'DAD.'

'Please, let me finish?' he asked. I nodded for him to carry on. 'But even I can't deny that you really have made a terrific effort since you've been,' he searched for the right words to say, 'been, er, released from prison. I'm not saying that I'm your new best friend but perhaps we could, you know, make more of an effort for the girls? It's obvious to me you two are pretty solid.' He looked at his hands. 'And after everything you've both been through, that has to be admired. I just don't want to be a thorn in all of this.' He looked embarrassed and surprisingly genuine.

'That's all I want, you know. I love Lily – that has never changed. And Lola. She is my whole world. Both of them mean everything to me. They're everything I've ever dreamed about. And I gotta say, you have done so much for them both and I've never thanked you for it – so thank you,' I said and held out my hand to shake his.

I looked at my hand, then at his. Slowly he reached out and we clutched hands in a firm shake. It wasn't a reunion of two long-lost pals but it was recognition of each other's importance in Lily and Lola's lives. It was a long overdue truce.

'Maybe I could take you out to dinner?'

'Dad, you know he hates it here,' Lily was still on edge.

'No,' I said, stopping Lily, 'that would be great.'

'If you'd rather, we'll come your end? Makes more sense as the girls are with you most of the time now, anyway.'

I looked at him; he really was making an effort. It knocked me for six. 'We can work something out, for sure.' We shook hands one last time, and then Lily and I got in the car. Lola was shouting, 'Granddad, Granddad,' as she pulled a face at him through the window. He tapped the window at her and smiled, before walking back inside.

'Whoa, what was all that about?' I said, smiling from ear to ear. It felt great.

'Don't know, but it seems . . .'

'Bloody fantastic. We got to go out with them – your parents. Show willing.' Lily was overjoyed with what had just happened, too. She hadn't seen it coming any more than I had.

'Mummy?'

'Yes, Lola?'

'Daddy said I could have a Happy Meal.'

Lily looked at me and I shrugged my shoulders, grinning like a Cheshire. She started the engine and we headed back – headed back home.

I ran though the dirty corridor of my bedsit with just a towel around me. It was freezing and I was dripping wet. I never got dressed in the showers. They were as fucking disgusting as the rest of the place. I opened the door to my room. It might not have been much, but it was heaven to me. Lily was sitting on the small two-seater sofa, sipping a glass of wine. Lola was tucked up in the camp bed, next to the double bed that I'd bought.

I'd spent a lot of time and money making it a really nice space. The room was big. The sleeping area was on the left, and the living area on the right. I'd got the bed off eBay for next to nothing, along with the nice dining table and widescreen TV with built-in DVD. Sure, they weren't brand new and were a little outdated, but with a bit of spit and polish, it all looked great. I had a nice thick rug on the floor and the sofa had come from the charity shop for free, as no one would pay for it. A good clean and a throw over the top to make it match the colour of the walls and it looked great. Lily and I had spent a long time making it all look lovely. I'd also bought a couple of electric heaters to keep it nice and warm for Lola. I made the money I did earn go as far as possible. I was saving for a flat – the housing association was helping me, as well, so I was hoping it wouldn't be too much longer.

'She's sleeping like a log – snoring and everything!' Lily remarked.

Lola looked like a little angel and she baby-snored.

'Good, that means we can, ya know, if we're quiet!' I leant down to kiss her.

We kissed passionately for a second, then she stopped and said, 'Oi, I'm starving – let's have our dinner first, Cain Thomas!' She wagged her finger at me, like a head mistress.

As I pulled back, her smile dropped a little as she saw the scars on my chest. She'd seen them many times before, but it always upset her to look at the physical wounds of my ugly past. They couldn't be hid. I changed the subject as I put on my clothes, 'Right, what we having?'

She had a load of menus on her lap. 'I really like this Chinese, but they don't take cards.' She gave it the puppy-dog eyes and all.

'Don't worry,' I said with a sigh, 'I'll nip into town and get some cash out.'

She clapped her hands in excitement. 'Take my card – you paid for the fuel.'

'Don't worry, I planned to!' She stuck her tongue out at me in jest.

'You make the order and I'll . . .'

'Hi, is that Hong Kong Chef?' She'd already dialled the number.

I was in town in less than five minutes. Loved that; so easy. Even though it was quarter to nine, the Hog's Head was heaving as I walked past. It was freezing cold. Bloody weather. I walked as quickly as I could; the pelican crossing was showing the green man so I jogged a little to catch it. Too late. I stood there waiting. My leg shook as I froze. The cash machine was just over the road, down a small side street. Finally, the green man, at last. I legged it across the road and down the side street. I dipped my hand in my pocket to retrieve my wallet. I was two paces or so away from the cash machine and was pleased no one was around – I could be quick and get back to my girls. I pulled out my card and felt someone tug my arm.

'Don't FUCKING move, blood. Your money from the machine NOW or you're dead.'

I looked around and two black lads, about sixteen or so, were standing there looking out of their fucking heads. Drooling, eyes wide and on edge.

'Boys, we ain't got to do this. Just turn around and walk away, yeah? Leave it.' They looked familiar. Fuck, where had I seen them?

BANG! One of them punched me in the face. 'Who the fuck you calling boys, huh? Your money now, you CUNT, or else.'

I rubbed the side of my face calmly. I knew not to make

any sudden movements, 'Fuck, I didn't mean that.' I should have remembered that I hated being called a boy. 'But this ain't happening, bruv,' I said to the talker. 'No chance. You're messing with the wrong bloke. Trust, just walk the fuck away, yeah?'

'YEAH?' he pulled out a blade. A fucking huge blade. It looked like some sort of fishing knife. I took a deep breath and slowly got myself into a fighting stance. I looked at them both through concentrated eyes.

Suddenly it came to me, 'I know you lads. Seen you, not for a while, though. Maldon Road bedsit? You were with a guy that lives there? Saw you the day I moved in. A year or so ago, yeah, remember?' I was trying to connect with them. Try the friend angle. They looked at each other, worried.

'Fuck that. Your money now, CUNT,' he said again, this time his hand holding the blade was shaking. Looked like his confidence was waning.

'Yeah, it was you two.' I felt like I was gaining some ground. 'Just forget this ever happened. We're sweet, yeah?'

Their heavy breathing slowed for a second as they looked at each other, weighing up the situation. His blade started to dip as he took his eyes off me and looked at his pal. I stared at the knife. Could I take it from him? I wasn't sure. Go on, GO ON. They whispered to each other. Suddenly, the one without the blade screamed, 'BUT HE FUCKING KNOWS US.'

Shit, this was going the wrong way. 'WHOA, WHOA,' I

shouted, 'that ain't no bad thing. Means you can just walk away, yeah, finish this now.'

'FUCK THAT,' shouted the bladeless boy.

He swung a punch at me, which I sidestepped, and then I planted a pucker left hook, knocking him straight into the cash machine. He quickly tried to come at me again but I whacked him for a second time, nearly knocking him off his feet. I had barely had time to take in what happened, when I felt two fucking big thuds to my lower back. It didn't so much hurt as made my legs buckle underneath me. I just about managed to stay on my feet, in a crouching position, trying to stand up straight. I looked around; the knifer came into view for a split second before he smashed me in the face, knocking me to the ground. The other boy had pulled himself together and they both began to stamp on me hard. I managed to protect my head as best I could with my arms, which were hammered instead. My torso and chest were battered.

'FUCKING PRICK,' were the last words I heard before they ran off.

My upper body was aching but I was OK. I wasn't knocked out and my head was sore but it didn't feel too bad. I went to get up but, as I did, I felt an electric shock of pain rip through both of my legs, like I was plugged into the mains, or something.

'ARRGGHH,' I screamed. It was excruciating.

My lower back began to pulse with pain. I was stuck on the floor, unable to move. I reached around to hold my lower back and try and ease the pain.

'Oh, God, no, please . . .' I felt two dirty great big puncture holes. They were soaking wet – it was as if two volcanoes had erupted on my back. As soon as I felt the wetness, I had to see it. I pulled my hand back and had a look.

'Jesus Christ, help me,' I muttered.

My hand was totally soaked in blood. It was a rich, dark red. Not a good sign.

'HELP! HELP ME!' I screamed.

The side street was dead. I tried to scramble to my feet once more but to no avail. I thought of Lily, sitting on the sofa, sipping her wine and watching Ant and Dec. Happy. Lola asleep. And here I was again, FUCKED. WHY? WHY? WHY? Suddenly, I remembered I had my mobile. I knew that I was bleeding like fuck. I couldn't move. I was scared. I dialled 999.

Through broken breaths I said, 'Ambulance. A FUCKING AMBULANCE. I'VE BEEN STABBED.' I started to panic. I felt my life slipping away and there was nothing I could do about it.

RUN

The sun was beautiful, it glistened on the seawater. The sand was pure white. So white, in fact, it practically blinded me when I looked at it. I'd never seen a sea so blue and waves as fluffy-white in all my life. Lily and Lola were down by the water's edge playing, motioning for me to go and join them. I felt the warm sun against my brow as I went down to be with them. The sand felt deep and it was difficult to walk. The more I tried, the harder it became. The harder it became, the more I tried. I was sinking. Stuck. Unable to move. Lily and Lola's smiles started to change. They looked worried. I was trying to get to them. Doing everything in my power. I was in paradise but I was sinking. Sinking fast. Unable to stop it. My girls. My beautiful girls. The fear on their faces. Lily screamed out, willing me to get to her. I couldn't stay up. I couldn't even get my feet out of the sand. Lola started to cry. I had to get to them. The sun became overcast, the place turned bleak. No matter how hard I tried, I couldn't get to them. Lily's screams turned into cries, she hugged our daughter with all her might, as I shouted in frantic insanity . . .

'Cain, CAIN?' Lily said.

'ARGH,' I screamed as I woke up.

I was covered in sweat, lying in a hospital bed. Like I had been for so, so long.

'You OK?' she asked. 'You were flinching and moving like crazy.'

'I was having that dream again. It's so vivid, Lil, like it's really happening.'

She squeezed my hand. 'I'm not going anywhere. Lola and I will be with you always.' She smiled. 'You just try and take us away.'

I tried to sit myself up but was struggling with every move. 'NO, I'm OK,' I said as Lily tried to help me.

It was difficult. I couldn't use my legs. I couldn't even feel them. I had been told not to worry by the doctors; told that it would take time before they could judge the extent of the damage. The weeks had ticked by and I'd been stuck in that bed, or stuck in the operating theatre, ever since the night I was stabbed. I was in prison all over again.

Lily had been brilliant. She'd come to see me every day. She brought Lola most of the time, as well. I'd even seen her parents and they both seemed genuinely upset about what had happened. Today, though, it was just Lily and me. I was about to get the verdict on the state of my legs and I only wanted her there with me.

'Why did you wake me?' I asked. Not that I wasn't pleased to see her, I just didn't sleep very well, so when I did fall asleep, I had to try and make the most of it, even if it was riddled with nightmares.

'The doctor popped his head in to say he'd be back in five minutes for a chat,' she said cautiously.

'The chat.' The one where I get read my sentence. Told what the quality of my life was going to be. As much as I wanted to know, I was dreading it. Lily and I sat there, not saying a word to each other. She was as nervous as I was. I looked at the clock every half a minute or so – the ticking was screwing with my mind. I just wanted him to hurry.

'Where the fuck is he?' I snapped.

'I'm here, Mr Thomas.' Shit, he'd walked in just as I said it.

'Oh, er, sorry, Doc – call me Cain,' I said with a nervous laugh. 'You've seen me enough times lately.'

He gave me a wrinkled and forced smile. He was in his mid-fifties, had a shaved head that was totally bald in the middle, trendy glasses and a sharp shirt and tie, with a Lacoste V-neck sweater over the top.

'Is it OK if I?' he nodded at the bed.

'Sure, Doc.' Good thing there was plenty of room; I didn't fancy trying to move again.

He sat down on the bed and flicked his clipboard over.

He started to look a little fidgety. 'Right, Cain, when you came in with your initial injuries, we did everything we could to stop the bleeding for a start and to close the wounds as quickly as possible to stop infection and to aid healing.' I nodded in agreement; Lily's eyes were glued to him. 'I told you from the outset that it was extremely difficult to see the level of damage caused by the stab wounds because of the swelling and tissue damage. It has been a lengthy road even to get to the stage when we can make a full evaluation and diagnosis. And, of course, prepare a treatment plan for you.'

'My legs, Doc. I still can't feel my legs?' I interrupted.

'I'm coming to that now. Obviously you have told us the pain you felt on impact and how you lost use of your legs. I made it clear from the start that temporary paralysis was something that can often happen in injuries like this. As your wounds have healed, though, and we've been able to carry out a number of tests and examinations on you—'

I was so nervous I couldn't stop myself jumping in, 'Pulled and prodded in every direction, more like.' I looked at Lily and laughed nervously, 'I've never known anything like it!' I tried to be light and cheerful – hoping it would bring me the good news I wanted. Needed.

The Doc smiled through closed lips and looked at me with sympathetic eyes. 'It was imperative that we did a full range of tests, to be sure that we came up with the best plan for care and support, so that you can live a full and comfortable life.'

My face became more serious. Lily put her hands to her mouth.

'What do you mean "care and support" for "a full and comfortable life"?' I was worried. Fucking scared out of my wits.

He took off his glasses, stroked his face and rugged chin. 'Cain,' he said softly, 'I said from day one that my biggest fear with your injuries was damage to your spinal cord. That was always my big worry. Damage to that, as I've told you, can have severe repercussions to one's mobility.'

'Oh, GOD, NO,' Lily shrieked as she began to cry.

I looked frantically back and forth between the doctor and Lily. 'What?' I asked. Please don't say it.

'I'm very sorry to have to tell you, but my worst fear is the reality. There's nothing else we can do.'

No, fuck no, this can't be happening. 'What . . . what do you mean there's nothing else you can do? You're a fucking doctor. You fix people, YOU CAN'T LEAVE ME LIKE THIS? A fucking cripple. A useless CUNT. PLEASE, DOC, help me.'

'I'm afraid your spinal cord was severed in the attack. It really is an injury that we are unable to repair at this stage.' Lily was hysterical. 'I know this is no consolation, but people in your situation really do live extremely comfortable lives these days and there are many support groups that will be able to help you come to terms with it.' He passed me a couple of leaflets that had pictures of disabled people smiling on the front. Smiling. 'And, like I said, spinal cord injuries can be fatal a lot of the time . . .'

I looked down at the leaflets and stared at the smiling faces in front of me. I felt rage, anger, hate. 'I'm not a FUCKING CRIPPLE, YOU HEAR?' I grabbed the leaflets and threw them back at him. He calmly let me have my moment.

'Please,' Lily begged though floods of tears, 'there must be something you can do. We have a daughter.' She was clutching at anything she could, to try to reverse the doctor's news.

'I'm sorry, I really am.'

My anger soon turned to desperation. 'Please, Doc, I'll do anything. Just help me. Please, I beg you.'

Although he must have delivered news like this many times before, it still can't have been an easy thing to do. 'There will be lots of help and we will monitor you and give you all the support in the world. Medicine advances all the time.' They were words of consolation, but Lily jumped on them.

'So maybe he will walk again?' she pleaded.

'I'm not saying that, and I can't say that. With the knowledge, skill and medicine available today, there is nothing that we can do for Cain's mobility. I'm just saying that you need to try and remain positive and look to the future in as best a light as you can. I will leave you two to be alone now. I'll leave the leaflets.' He looked at me in the eyes. 'Once again, Cain, I'm terribly sorry. I really am.' He was genuine – but, one thing's for sure, he was nowhere near as sorry as I was.

I looked at Lily, totally gobsmacked. Guilt soon followed, 'Maybe if I'd run away, or . . . or, maybe if I'd given them money. Or not told them I knew them.' Over and over it played out in my mind.

I hadn't been trying to be a hero. I just did what I thought was the right thing to do while under pressure, with a knife being waved in my face. Was I right or wrong? Only God knows that. But I couldn't help thinking that if I had made another choice that night, I might have WALKED away to tell the tale.

Lily moved in closer to me. Tight as she could, putting her head on my chest and cuddling me. I felt my chest get saturated from her tears. I kissed the top of her head and pulled her in closer. One lonely tear trickled down my cheek as I held her. I was destroyed. I knew that I was never going to be able to walk again.

PEACE TRAIN

I was really building up some pace. My shoulders and arms burnt like a bugger. I'd been out running for nearly two hours. Only this was a different type of running – I had one of the best marathon wheelchairs around. The college combined with a bit of fundraising had helped me buy some amazing kit. I was totally exhausted as I turned into my road and raced up to the two-bedroom bungalow I now lived in with Lily and Lola. I was hoping she'd started cooking some tea, because I was damn hungry.

I'm twenty-three years old and I really have lived a life less than ordinary. I had a confused and difficult start in life. That's a fact and not a self-pitying statement. I've learnt to come to terms with things in my past that were out of my control. My early childhood being one of them. The sexual abuse I suffered at the hands of a predator stained me, in every sense of the word.

However, I'm still accountable for the bad things I did. I'm a human being who made some sick and violent choices. Even though I've had some terrible things happen to me, I should have been strong enough to choose a different path, instead of inflicting my wrath on the world. But I say this without guilt or apprehension. I was failed also. I didn't have any parents. I became a problem for the State. And I was failed by them. I'm not shirking my responsibility here, but if I'd had just a tiny bit of help and understanding, it might have helped me be a better kid. The more I got moved from pillar to post, the more difficult and horrible I became. You might ask, why didn't I stop being horrible? I'm talking about when I was five, six, seven, eight years old. A baby. A child. Looking back, it was my call for help. I'm not saying it was right, or that some of my actions were excusable, but I was a baby. And, I'm sorry to say, the system MUST take some responsibility for the total screw-up I became.

There isn't a day that goes by, even now, in which TJ doesn't enter my thoughts. I truly am sorry for what happened. It was tragic and sad, and several people were destroyed because of it. And I don't just mean physically.

Prison is a concrete reality for some kids. If you push the buttons hard enough. I never thought I'd hear myself say this, but they are getting tougher to press. Violence and destruction on the streets is getting worse, not better. I'm not saying prison is the answer, necessarily. I had some bad times in there but I was also lucky enough to meet some incredible people, such as Mr Byrd. More people like him and this world would be a better place, of that I'm sure. But something does have to be done. Kids are killing each other on a daily basis and they're doing it like it means nothing. A small scrap behind the bike sheds. It's a worrying thought for the future. Going through what I've been through and, of course, now that I am a father, I think I'm qualified to have an opinion. I've seen it, lived it and got the T-shirt.

Mrs June and I still write to one another. Every month or so. Lily contacted her to tell her about the attack on me and about losing the use of my legs. She came to see me as soon as she heard and has offered support on every level. You may think it's strange after what happened between TJ and me. But tragedy can have a profound effect on us human beings. Deep down, there probably is a caring and forgiving part in most of us. And when you are forced to face tragedy, it makes you see things differently and, ultimately, your humanity is tested. Mrs June is a wonderful woman.

After that day in the hospital, the greatest struggle of our lives began. Some things I do need to keep for myself – this isn't a story about my rehabilitation from a knife attack. Of course, it is an integral part of who I am now and what I've been through on my journey – but I refuse to wallow in it. I'm not here to make you feel sorry for me because I'm disabled. My story is one of pain, anger and regret. A path that has followed the deepest lows and climbed the highest heights. Being attacked – stabbed – really did put me into the shoes of a victim for real. I saw in those boys EXACTLY what I had seen in the mirror as a teenager. And that is my concern – youngsters are killing at the drop of a hat. He tried to kill me, just because I refused to give him money and I told him I recognised him. Because of that, I have to live my life in a wheelchair.

The two boys were caught doing another robbery. They were charged and convicted for what they did to me. I didn't go to court. Didn't see the point. But I bet they couldn't give a toss right now. They will. One day they really will.

The college was great – they did everything in their power to help me. I'm going to start a degree in graphic design – I could never have imagined it possible. Tom was a godsend and helped me every step of the way. And when he asked if he could show Shark-Boy to one of his colleagues that day, what he hadn't told me was that his colleague worked at a graphic novel publishing company. He loved my idea. The one thing I've learnt is that there're no guarantees in life, but this guy and I have been developing the story as a graphic novel for a few years. Who knows what may come of it?

When I was told I'd never use my legs again, I thought my fitness and training were finished. Caput. How wrong

I was! The gym where I worked kept my job open, and I still do it to this day. Admittedly, I'm restricted in what I can do, but they thought that my knowledge, advice and abilities still had a place in their gym. They were also instrumental in helping to keep my spirits up and encouraging me to train for wheelchair marathons – which I am doing. I've done two half marathons and will take part in my first full marathon very soon.

Lily, Lola and I live in a nice, quiet part of town. The bungalow has all the facilities I need in my condition, plus more. We are engaged and hoping to get married in a couple of years. Her parents have been supportive. Lola is seven. A proper little madam in every sense of the word! Maybe one day we'll have some more kids. Who knows?

I've lived through some of the worst things imaginable and most of them came about because of juvenile idiocy. If just one person looks at me, listens to my words and changes their life, then mine, for all its faults, will have been for some good.

I have a beautiful partner and the best daughter in the world. Given the circumstances, it is a miracle. And, because of them, I really am the happiest man alive. Believe.

BANGED UP

RONNIE THOMPSON

'Hard hitting and powerful' John King,
author of *The Football Factory*

DRUG DEALS. GANG FIGHTS. BLOODSHED.
And that's after he was sent down.

Davey Sommers had the start in life many could only
wish for – a middle-class boy from a respectable,
hard-working family. But he quickly descended into a
life of drugs, violence and intimidation, becoming
the 'big man' and eventually serving a seventeen-year
sentence for his crimes.

In *Banged Up* Ronnie Thompson teams up with
Davey Sommers to reveal the brutality of life behind
bars. From the realities of being a 'face' in prison
to the violent conditions that drove Davey to attempt
a life on the run, this is the gritty story of the rise
and fall of a criminal, and a shockingly honest
account of life as a con.

NON-FICTION / MEMOIR 978 0 7553 1987 9

More Non-fiction from Headline

SCREWED

RONNIE THOMPSON

'Honest, brutal, gripping' Garry Bushell

DRUGS. VIOLENCE. CORRUPTION.

And that's just the screws.

My name is Ronnie Thompson. Being a Prison Officer for Her Majesty's Prison Service was something I used to be proud of. I soon realised the truth of what it's like working as a screw – the danger, pressures, duties, life-wrecking conditions – a fucking headache.

Ronnie Thompson tells it like it is. For the first time ever, a Prison Officer reveals what really goes on behind bars.

He exposes the underworld of bent screws, the drugs they traffic, the firms they work for and what they get paid for their sins. He talks about the times when force is necessary and used, and when it is unnecessary but still used.

Ultimately, he shows that being a good screw doesn't always mean sticking to the rules . . .

NON-FICTION / Memoir 978 0 7553 6265 3